"Nicola M... communicate scie... ...e biology ...ain to the general reader in a way that will not only ... but entertain."
**...ssor Simon Baron-Cohen, *Department of Developmental ...opathology, Cambridge University***

...! It taught me a lot about my brain..."
**...Rae, *age 13***

...me a lot about my son!"
**...e Rae, *age 45***

...o say how much I enjoyed the book. It is excellent and just ...needed."
**...ssor John Stein, *Oxford University***

...for teenagers but invaluable reading for those coping with ...parents, doctors, and teachers – *Blame My Brain*, ...to the biology behind teenage behaviour, is informative, ...le, interactive, and fun... Our practice has a books-on-...tion scheme. I am going to suggest that we get six copies ...ook. In fact, maybe I'll suggest that we get a copy for every ...the practice."
***Medical Journal***

...y rare that an author succeeds in writing a book for ...s which is also a 'must read' for their parents and teachers. ...organ has done just that. *Blame My Brain* does not ...xcuse teenage behaviour, but it certainly goes a long ...xplaining it."
**...otsman**

...d resource to share with students to help them deal with ...otentially the most challenging, but also the most exciting, ...their development."
***...ducational Supplement***

# Books by the same author

# NICOLA MORGAN

# BLAME MY BRAIN
## THE
# AMAZING
# TEENAGE
# BRAIN
## REVEALED

WALKER BOOKS
AND SUBSIDIARIES

LONDON • BOSTON • SYDNEY • AUCKLAND

First published 2005 by Walker Books Ltd
87 Vauxhall Walk, London SE11 5HJ

This edition published 2013

6 8 10 9 7

Text © 2005, 2013 Nicola Morgan
Illustrations pages 11, 17, 18, 29, 126, 142, 143, 144 © 2005 Andy Baker

The right of Nicola Morgan and Andy Baker to be identified as author and
illustrator respectively of this work has been asserted by them
in accordance with the Copyright, Designs and Patents Act 1988

This book has been typeset in Clarendon, Ionic and Shinn

Printed in Great Britain by Clays Ltd, St Ives plc

British Library Cataloguing in Publication Data:
a catalogue record for this book is available from the British Library

ISBN: 978-1-4063-4693-0

www.walker.co.uk

**To my daughters.**
**If only I'd known all this sooner!**

# Acknowledgements

As I say elsewhere, I am not a scientist. But real scientists generously gave their time and expertise, and made this book possible. I approached them nervously for help or advice, assuming that they would be too busy, or perhaps that they would be dismissive of a science book written by a non-scientist. Instead, I was overwhelmed by their generosity, support and enthusiasm. For their encouragement, or help, or very often both, I would like to express my huge gratitude to Professor Simon Baron-Cohen, Professor Sarah-Jayne Blakemore, Dr Stephanie Burnett Heyes, Dr Paul Ekman, Professor Susan Greenfield, Dr Murray Johns, Professor John Stein, Dr Deborah Yurgelun-Todd and Professor Marvin Zuckerman. Of course, the views I express in the book are not necessarily theirs and any mistakes are entirely mine.

# Contents

*If the human brain was simple enough to understand,*
*we'd be too simple to understand it.*
Emerson Pugh,[1] 1977

## A note from the author: why this new edition?

Because now we know even more than when I wrote the first edition and I'm so fascinated by it that I had to tell you! I also wanted to check everything against our new knowledge. Since *Blame My Brain* was first published in 2005, scientists around the world have been doing more and more research, which adds to what we knew. There's new information on emotional processing, pruning of connections, risk-taking, sleep, and alcohol and drugs. And I will introduce you to the fascinating world of mirror neurons. In short, with this edition, teenagers and all the adults who care about them can know even more about why adolescence can be such a stressful and tumultuous time, as well as an incredibly important one.

# Introduction

All parents were once perfect teenagers. Model humans. Never drank, smoked, swore or lay in bed all morning. They were completely in control of all their hormones. In fact, they probably never had any hormones at all. They were calm, always smiling and incredibly polite to everyone around them.

All parents also have amnesia. That's why they think the above paragraph is true.

They have airbrushed out the disgusting bits of their memories. The painful, greasy, smelly, hormonal, angry, nasty bits. They will tell you they tidied their rooms and filed away the day's school work alphabetically before supper each evening. *And* brought in the coal during winter and chopped logs in the forest and sold matches on the frozen streets to make enough money for a trip to the library as a special treat. If they'd even dreamt of swearing at an adult, they would have been forced to write out five million times: "I have unquestioning respect for all adults." Exams were harder and they were cleverer because there were no videos/PlayStations/computers/Internet in their day. They were all poor but happy. And on Christmas Day, their greatest joy was to play family charades. After writing their thank-you letters. Brussels sprouts? No, they didn't like them but they always ate them and appreciated their traditional importance. Sprouts are character-building.

If adults only knew the truth about the teenage brain, they'd realize that they couldn't have escaped its special behaviour. If they read this book, they might begin, gradually, to remember the truth about their teenage years. What they don't realize, and what this book sets out to show, is that the teenage brain has always been special. Different, fascinating and important things are happening inside it, which happen to everyone. Some of this is new information, or supports what scientists have recently known. Most adults will be surprised, fascinated and reassured by the contents of this book.

I want to give you a behind-the-scenes look into your own brain, so next time you're facing a row for not getting out of bed before lunch or not going to bed before dawn, for swearing at a teacher, for smoking even though it's bad for you, for reacting emotionally, for taking risks, for generally being stroppy, you could just say, "Don't blame me – blame my brain."

Actually, none of this is exactly an excuse: it's an explanation. Once you know what's going on in your brain and why, you can work *with* your brain instead of being so stressed out by it. Knowledge and understanding are half the battle.

You might even decide to respect your brain and treat it a bit better, once you know what's going on inside it.

Read on and be amazed.

*Nicola Morgan*
*Edinburgh, 2013*

# Brain Basics

There are a few things you need to know so that the rest of the book makes sense. You need some basic facts about brains and how they work. Then, when I use a word like **neuron** later, you'll know what I'm on about. And if you forget, you can come back to this section.

### BRAIN BASIC 1: WHAT'S IN A BRAIN?

The human brain contains about 100 billion nerve cells (neurons). Each neuron has a long tail-like part (**axon**) and many branches (**dendrites** – from the Greek word *dendron*, meaning tree). A neuron sends super-fast messages to other neurons by passing a tiny electrical

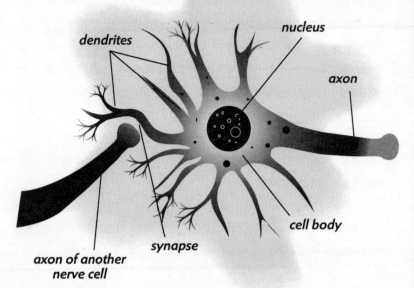

nucleus

dendrites

axon

cell body

synapse

axon of another
nerve cell

current along its axon and across very tiny gaps (**synapses**) into the dendrites of other neurons.

If the neurons did not communicate, your body would do nothing. Every single thing you do – every thought, action, sneeze, emotion, even things like going to the toilet – happens when the neurons send the right messages, very fast, through this incredibly complicated web of branches.

Each time you repeat the same action, or thought, or recall the same memory, that particular web of connections is activated again. Each time that happens, the web of connections becomes stronger. And the stronger the connections, the better you are at that particular task. That's why practice makes perfect.

But if you don't use those connections again, they may die off. That's how you forget how to do something – forget a fact or a name, or how to do a maths calculation, or how to kick a ball at a perfect angle. If you want to relearn anything, you have to rebuild your web of connections – by practising again. After a brain injury, such as a stroke, someone might have to relearn how to walk or speak. That would be if the stroke had damaged some neurons and dendrites which help to control walking or speaking.

We all have different skills. The brains of a pianist and a footballer will have different numbers of dendrites and synapses in different areas of their brains.

When a human baby is born, it has almost all of its neurons. But it has few dendrites and therefore few synapses connecting them. That is why babies can't do very much. But their brains develop fast. The fastest time of dendrite development in a baby is at around 8 months. Eventually, there can be up to 100,000 dendrites on every neuron, making 100 trillion connections.

The brain is made of **grey matter** and **white matter**. Grey matter is mainly made up of neurons and you find most of it in the **cortex** (the outer wrinkly bit of the brain, which is only about 2 millimetres thick). White matter is mostly below the cortex and is made up of all the axons that carry messages between neurons. We could call grey matter the "clever stuff". But it couldn't do very much if there wasn't plenty of good strong white matter too.

You also have brain cells called **glial cells**. These can't carry messages or make you do anything, but they support and nourish the neurons and help remove debris.

### BRAIN BASIC 2: MIRROR NEURONS

There is a fascinating type of neuron called a **mirror neuron**. These were first identified by scientists in Italy[2] in the 1990s and they are beginning to offer real insights into how we all learn. When we do something, neurons in the relevant part of our brain fire up, sending messages to enable us to act. But some of our neurons – mirror neurons – fire up when we simply watch someone else perform an action.

Those same mirror neurons will also be used when we perform the action ourselves. So, if we watch someone do something a few times, when we come to do it ourselves it may be easier because some of our neurons have already actually practised the action. Some scientists believe that mirror neurons have a role to play in empathy – feeling what others feel.

So, how the people around us behave should be very important for how we behave – and that's not just for young people, but people of all ages. It helps explain how we learn by imitation.

### BRAIN BASIC 3: MAKING CONNECTIONS

The connections do not happen of their own accord. Or randomly. Connections grow when we do something. Each time a baby tries to focus on an object, this makes connections multiply and then strengthen in the parts of the brain which deal with seeing. *And* in the parts which deal with understanding what we see. *And* in the parts that deal with remembering what we have seen.

Scientists can look at the brains of young rats and actually count increased dendrites after the rats have, for example, spent some days learning their way around a maze.[3]

14

I think it's also interesting (though perhaps a bit frightening) to know that scientists have also discovered that there are critical periods in a brain's development and that if the brain doesn't get the right practice at the right time, it may not be able to learn certain skills later. That's why, if you don't learn a foreign language before the age of about 7, you *could* still learn to speak it fluently but you'll probably always speak it with the wrong accent, because you have passed the stage at which the brain can pick up accents. It's also why, if a baby doesn't have an opportunity to use its eyes properly at around 8 months old, its sight will never develop properly later.[4] But, luckily for us, most skills are not like this: *most* skills can be picked up later even if we miss out on some early learning.

If you think of your brain cells and connections as being like trees, it's easier to picture what's going on. Imagine starting with a very simple tree with a few branches – if you water and feed it, it will grow lots more branches. That's a bit like what happens when you do or practise something – it develops the brain cells which are responsible for that particular thing. And makes them grow more branches, or stronger branches.

### BRAIN BASIC 4: BRAIN ZONES

Although each human is a unique individual, our brains all have the same areas or sections, all working roughly in the same way (though there are some wonderful differences when you look very, very closely at the way individual brains work).

Different parts of the brain help control the different types of activity we do, but it's not quite as simple as saying, "This part controls memory and this part controls movement." There are different types of memory and different types of movement, and how good you are at memory or movement will depend on how well all the parts of your brain connect and how strong the branches or pathways are between them. One way of understanding this is to think about playing the piano: to play the piano, you need to use your memory of how to play the piano *and* your memory for the notes of a particular piece *and* the ability to control movement of several parts of your body *and* the bits of the brain that control sight – *and* the bits that specifically control your fingers. Playing the piano involves several parts of your brain all working together.

So, later in this book I'll sometimes (quite often, actually!) mention a part of the brain called the **prefrontal cortex** and I'll say that it "includes the bits that control logic, decision-making, complex thinking" – but it is in fact more complicated than that, because lots of bits of the brain will be working together. And there's still a lot that scientists don't yet know about how all the parts work together.

*But,* we can still say that particular parts of the brain are especially important for particular activities.

16

The next picture shows you the main brain parts and the main things they help control. You have two halves to your brain and each half looks very similar to the other half and has matching sections. They are connected, and for most activities you use both halves together but in slightly different ways.

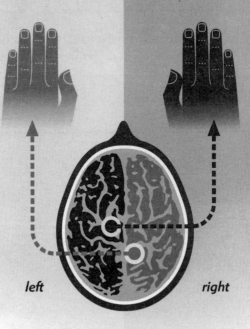

The left half of your brain controls everything on the right side of your body, and the right half controls your left side.

*left*                    *right*

# A BRAIN MADE SIMPLE

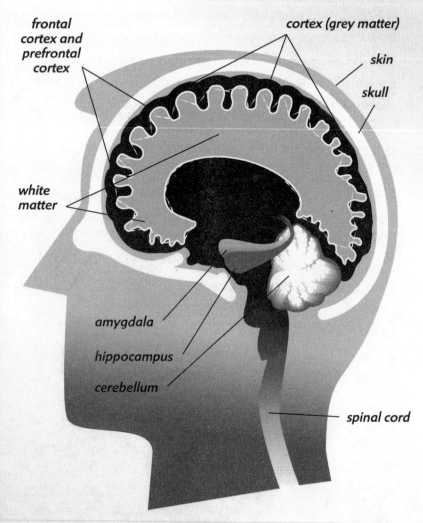

frontal cortex and prefrontal cortex

cortex (grey matter)

skin

skull

white matter

amygdala

hippocampus

cerebellum

spinal cord

## BRAIN BASIC 5: THE THREE-YEAR MYTH

Scientists *used* to think that:

- we are born with all the neurons we'll ever have and that no more grow – WRONG
- almost all the brain's growth and development happens by about the age of 3, and hardly any dendrites or connections grow after this – WRONG
- after the age of 5 or 6, neurons start dying and are never replaced – WRONG

This is known as the "three-year myth" – the *wrong* belief that all important development is done in the first three years and after that it is downhill all the way.

We now know that the brain continues to develop and even to grow more neurons later in our lives, too. Yes, older adults can learn new skills, making new connections between existing cells and sometimes growing new neurons. And, importantly for you, we know that **adolescence** is a time of major change in the volume of grey matter, and that some parts of your brain are affected more than others.

## BRAIN BASIC 6: WINDOWS INTO THE BRAIN

How do we suddenly know so much more about the human brain? Our increasing knowledge comes from technology that allows scientists to see inside a living, conscious brain, without risk to the brain's owner. Before, the only ways of examining a human brain were to dissect it or to use scanning techniques which involved things like injecting radioactive dye into people. This meant that scientists didn't have the chance to examine healthy brains and couldn't scan the same person over and over again, because the techniques could be harmful. Also, the old methods couldn't say anything about what was happening in the brain while the person was doing something.

Everything changed when a new technique came along: functional magnetic resonance imaging (fMRI). This allows researchers to examine what is happening in someone's brain while they perform any particular activity. If you had your brain scanned using fMRI, we'd see exactly what parts of your brain were being used during a particular activity.

Because fMRI is harmless, scientists can now scan, measure and compare the brains of healthy, active teenagers. At first, they were amazed by what they saw and they are still finding more fascinating and detailed insights into the brains of adolescents. The teenage brain really is special.

## A Word About Genes

Actually, I'm not going to talk about genes at all in this book. Some people might find that a bit odd. After all, our genes (as well as our environment and the things that happen to us) make us who we are and have an enormous part to play in what our brains are like. They are the codes which we inherit from our parents (and other more distant ancestors) and which can be found in all cells in our bodies. They make you different from me and more like your brother or sister than anyone else in the world. But they are not relevant to this book, which talks about how teenage brains in general are like other teenage brains and unlike the brains of older or younger people. You can blame your genes as well, if you like – in other words, your parents. And grandparents. And all sorts of dead people you never knew. But it's not nearly so interesting as looking inside your own head.

# CHAPTER ONE

# Powerful Emotions

*"I hate you — oh, and by the way,*
*can I have some money?"*

*Meet Matt. And his mum. There is an emotional war*
*going on. And neither of them knows why.*

Matt's parents are worried about him. He used to be a model pupil but recently his grades have slipped. He is moody, spends a lot of time in his room, and listens to dreadful music with lyrics which are negative, depressed and frankly weird. He has posters of Kurt Cobain around his room and when his mum asked politely why he liked Kurt Cobain his answer was: "Because, like, he killed himself and that is just SO neat."

"Unlike your room," she joked, trying not to react.

"God, Mum, you're always going *on*. Just leave me alone!" he shouted, giving her an odd manic glare. Was he on drugs? she wondered.

Anyway, yes, so they are worried about him. They only want him to be happy. And safe. And nice to them. And successful. And an A-grade student. And get a brilliant job. And score more goals than anyone else in the inter-schools football tournament when everyone is watching. Yes, they are worried about Matt. But it's only because they *care*. It's a tough world out there and how will he get on if he shouts at his parents? Will he shout at his employers too? Will he be a complete failure? It's enough to drive a mother to breaking point herself.

So, this evening, Matt's mum has decided to have a little chat. Just a relaxing chat about nothing in particular. A chance to do some mother-son bonding. She's going to go into his room and ask how his day was. No pressure.

She knocks on the door. No reply. Again, louder. No reply. So she turns the handle, at the same time calling his name. The room is quite dark. There's a smell of incense. But she will ignore that. It's quite a nice smell, actually. Soothing. Though no amount of dry-cleaning will ever get it out of the curtains. And she made those curtains herself, sewed till her fingers bled, to make the house look beautiful, and what does Matt care? She pushes aside the shiver of teeth-grinding irritation.

"Matt," she calls. He is lying on his bed, eyes closed, headphones wrapped around his head, drumming the beat on his mattress. His homework is lying open on the desk. Peering through the gloom, she reads the title: "To what extent was Macbeth's downfall within his control?" He has written two lines so far: "In the play *Macbeth* by William Shakespeare, Macbeth has a very tragic downfall. It was entirely the witches' fault because they shouldn't of ever said what they said." Crammed into the margin are detailed doodles and when she looks closely she sees they are dozens of hangman's nooses all entwined together.

She moves the burning incense to a safer place and accidentally kicks over a can of Coke on the floor. Matt opens his eyes.

"Mum! What the hell are you doing? This is my room! Get out! OK?"

"Yes, sorry, Matt. I did knock."

"Yeah, well, knock louder next time."

"I just thought I'd come and ask how your day was. Can I get you anything? I could bring you some tea or something. It's quite a good idea to drink tea while you're doing your homework. Relaxing and stimulating at the same time."

"Yeah, well, I'm not doing homework, am I?"

"Don't you think you should finish this essay?" she says, pointing at the almost empty page.

Matt rips his headphones off and with exaggerated effort hauls himself to his feet. He is six inches taller than his mum and looking down on her is a great feeling. "Look, butt out, Mum. It doesn't need to be done for ages."

"When?"

"Like, days. I don't know, Friday or something."

"Don't you even know?"

"Yes, it's written down. It's under control. I'm not stupid, you know."

"Well, OK, but how about doing some other homework then? There must be something that needs to be done for tomorrow. It's a good idea to try to be ahead of things, Matt. Don't you get weekly French tests? I could test you or something. It's so much easier to learn when someone tests you." She picks up a book from a pile on the floor.

You can almost see the electricity fizzing through Matt's body. You can see the anger in his clenched muscles and his thunderous face.

"Put it down, Mum. Leave me alone! I'll do it by myself. You don't know any French anyway."

"Well, if you *will* do it on your own, fine, Matt. But will you? That's what I want to know!"

"Oh, right, so you don't trust me now?"

"Well, I want to trust you. But how can I trust you after last week, when I found that message in your notebook from Mrs Legless saying you hadn't done your homework?"

"That was just once!"

"And the week before? Mr Golightly?"

"That was because you made me do the ****** housework!"

"No, Matt. You have your chores to do at the weekend and you know the deal is that if you don't do them then, you have to do them during the week."

"It's unfair. No one else has to do chores. Why does the house have to be so bloody tidy anyway? What are you? A cleaning obsessive? Even my friends think this house is weird cos it's so clean. There's medical treatment for people like you – I was reading about it the other day. There's even a name for it. It's a mental disorder. You should see a doctor."

"That's enough, Matt!" shouts his mother. "Don't speak to me like that!"

A voice shouts irritably from downstairs. Matt's dad. "What's going on, you two? Keep the noise down, for goodness' sake! I can't hear myself think."

Matt looks at his mum triumphantly. She fumes, betrayed, furious. And it had all started with her offering to help.

She picks up some dirty socks and leaves the room. Matt slams the door.

"Don't slam the door!" she shouts.

"Get out of my life!" he yells back.

Five minutes later he comes downstairs.

"There's a party at someone's house on Saturday. Not sure where. I need new jeans. Can I have some money?"

## What's going on in Matt's brain?

Why does a previously sensible, happy boy, who was ticking along quite nicely, working reasonably hard, being reasonably nice to his parents, suddenly turn into someone whose anger erupts like a volcano at the slightest hint of intrusion? Why the arguments that blow up out of nothing? And why does Matt feel lousy inside with that eternal cry of "It's not fair!"?

Experts used to say, "It's just **hormones**", or "It's just a natural desire to break free from parents and move towards independence." Both those things are partly true. But new research shows something very special going on in the teenage brain.[5] Something which makes it work in a different way – something which even makes it look different inside from either a child's brain or an adult brain.

Before you read on, remember two things: first, not all teenagers go through this difficult emotional phase. Second, teenagers are not the only people who can be irrational and emotional, volatile, argumentative and snappy. Ever look at the adults around you? What's their excuse for rattiness and foul temper? They would probably say that YOU are their excuse. Hmm.

Previously we thought that teenage humans were the only ones to go through adolescence, but when scientists looked at other mammals, like rats and monkeys, they

27

found similar changes in the brain and similar changes in behaviour. Maybe rats feel ratty too.

What about Matt and his arguments? What's this got to do with our new knowledge about teenage brain changes?

Scientists are careful about drawing conclusions. They say: "We see these changes in the brain and we see these changes in behaviour: they *might* be linked but we can't be sure exactly how." They're right to be cautious – scientists are supposed to be cautious – but let's look at what we see, because it is fascinating. And all the scientists agree on THAT.

First, we see a major increase of grey matter in the prefrontal cortex – the part of the brain that has most to do with thinking, reasoning, logic, decision-making. It is like a tree suddenly growing and branching out in the spring. This increase mainly happens just before **puberty**, usually between the ages of 10 and 12. The peak of grey matter growth is at around 11 years for girls and 12 for boys. In fact, far too many connections or synapses grow at this stage (which is also what happens in a young baby's brain). They will need to be cut back, or pruned, which is what happens next.

After the huge growth which happens just before and at the start of puberty, you have a period during adolescence where the branches are cut back or pruned. It's as though the cells the brain doesn't need just fall away. Scientists think that this pruning is more important than the growth, like pruning a tree to make its branches fewer but thicker and stronger. By the age of 16 or 17 you have adult levels of synapses – but when you were 1 or 2 you had twice as many.

During normal adolescence you lose around 15% of grey matter from your cortex. Then, in late adolescence and into early adulthood, the brain spends time building up and thickening the branches that are left, coating the axons to make them strong. This strengthening stage is called myelination. There is more about it in Chapter Six.

*child*

*early puberty*

*middle of puberty*

*end of puberty*

Adolescence is a period of huge and surprising physical change in the brain. It is as though many different parts are being remodelled to work in the more complex ways necessary in adult life. And during this upheaval and change, maybe the pathways for sensible behaviour are just not working well.

In support of this theory, researchers have found something else very interesting about Matt's brain. It's time you took the teenager test.

Look at the picture opposite.

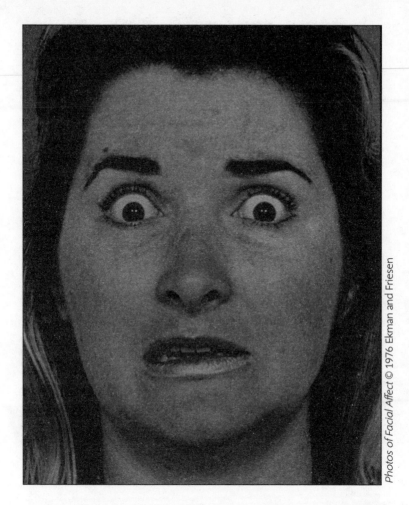

Photos of Facial Affect © 1976 Ekman and Friesen

What emotion do you think this person is showing? What is she feeling? Think about it for a few seconds.

Now turn the page.

## WHAT DID YOU SAY?

Did you say any of these:

Anger? Shock? Disgust? Pain?

If you said any or all of these, you are just like many teenagers, but you are also *completely* wrong.

The person in the picture is showing one emotion, and one only. And that is *fear*. Or you could call it terror. But it is *not* anger, or shock, or disgust.

In an experiment researchers asked a group of adults and adolescents the same question.[6] Quite simply, *all* the adults got it right and a large number of the adolescents got it wrong.

Amazingly, when the researchers scanned the brains of the participants, they discovered that most of the teenagers were using different parts of their brain when they looked at the picture.

When adults looked at the picture, the part of the brain which showed activity was mainly in the prefrontal cortex – that sensible bit which tells you not to order your mother to get out of your life if you want her to give you some money.

When adolescents like Matt looked at the picture, the part of the brain which seemed to be working overtime was the **amygdala**. This is a tiny part linked to gut reaction, raw emotion. The amygdala is one area of the brain which is almost fully developed in a baby – it works through instinct, not logic. It is not a thinking part at all.

Dr Deborah Yurgelun-Todd, the researcher who discovered this interesting behaviour, suggests that this *may* mean that teenagers have difficulty reading the faces of the adults around them – they may think an adult is showing anger when it is worry and concern, or disgust when it is simply surprise. She found that boys are also slightly worse than girls at this, and seemed to be using their emotional amygdala more strongly. The research is still going on, and even more interesting things may yet be discovered. Some research suggests that 11-12 year olds are 15% slower than younger children at matching the emotion on a face to the emotion word, and that this ability doesn't recover fully until about the age of 16. (This result hasn't been repeated, so it may turn out to be different when more research is done, but it does seem that many young adolescents have particular problems with this task.)

Now, we can't say, "We see this in the brain, *therefore* teenagers are reacting emotionally instead of logically." Brains are not that easy to understand. What we can say is, "The teenagers get it wrong and seem to be using a different part of the brain *while* they are getting it wrong."

It makes you think, though. Is the way Matt's brain is currently wired up affecting the way he interprets his mother's face and voice? Is he misreading her signals? Is he unable to work out that, actually, she does want the best for him, *is* concerned about him, does want to help him? Yes, she's nagging horribly, but does his teenage brain make it impossible to understand and to do what he knows he should: which is to do his homework before the deadline? Is this why he can't see beyond his gut reaction of fury, a feeling of invasion, a need to shout "Get out of my life"?

Psychologists say that there are 412 separate emotions which humans can feel, each of which we express on our faces. If you want to see how good you are at telling what someone is feeling, try the test at the end of this chapter.

Mind you, let's remember that parents can also be emotional, furious, illogical, irritating, irrational, uncontrolled, plain stupid. And regret it afterwards if they've got any sort of decency. Wouldn't it be interesting to see an fMRI scan of what's going on in a parent's brain during arguments with teenage offspring?

A possible theory about what is going on in Matt's brain is this: the early teenage brain is changing its structure. First it increases in density and number of connections, far more than it needs, especially in the prefrontal cortex. Then it does massive pruning, losing connections in some areas and restructuring itself in ways we do not yet understand. And Matt hasn't reached the final stage of strengthening myelination yet.

Matt's behaviour could be affected by all this change, and this is perhaps partly why he behaves like the "typical teenager". Personally, I can't see how he could *avoid* being affected. After all, it's our brains that make us feel the way we do.

Apart from anything else, Matt is probably under stress from many things going on in his life – friendships, pressure at school, exams, fears for the future – and stress does make us more ratty, more snappy. Add that to what's going on in his brain, and you have a recipe for volatility.

## Other emotional brain differences

Recent studies have shown other differences between teenage and adult brains when they think about emotional situations. For example, research[7] shows teenagers and adults using different parts of the brain when thinking of socially embarrassing situations. Interestingly, some studies[8] show areas of the prefrontal cortex working *harder* in teenagers than in adults for some activities. So, it's not at all the case that your prefrontal cortex is sleepy: just that it works differently and may produce different results.

## Hormones

What about hormones? Hormones are the chemicals which adults for generations have blamed for all teenage mood swings. Well, hormones are certainly still guilty. We know very well that they affect mood and therefore behaviour very directly, and we know very well that hormones are racing madly around the bodies of teenagers, turning them from children to adults within a few years. Scientists now also believe that hormones can change the physical structure of your brain too.

But what controls the hormones? The brain. We are not sure what triggers puberty, but it is certainly something in the brain that tells those hormones to start racing. Hormones and changes within the brain are linked in complicated ways, but what *is* certain is that both are particularly important during adolescence.

There's more about the effects of hormones in Chapter Four.

## Why do we have adolescence? And why is it so much longer in humans than in other animals?

We now know that some other mammals have a period of adolescence, too, including monkeys, rats and mice. New research in the US on macaque monkeys[9] has shown more clearly than before that neurons and synapses are pruned away during adolescence, as they are in humans. Those mammals that have a period of adolescence get through it much more quickly than humans. The female rhesus monkey goes from puberty to adulthood between the ages of around 18 and 48 months – and displays many equivalent characteristics, including teenage sleeping patterns, risk-taking and spending huge amounts of time hanging out with other adolescent monkeys.[10] Maybe they even do the monkey equivalent of swearing at their parents.

Here are some ideas about why humans need a relatively long adolescence and why it's the emotional ride that it is. They are not separate possibilities but are closely linked together. For example, evolution is responsible for our biological make-up, and our biology in turn leads to the way we behave as a society. So don't look at them as separate theories, but just as different ways to focus your thoughts.

### THEORY 1 – IT'S EVOLUTION

An evolutionary biologist always looks at questions like this by saying: "This must have given some advantage to early humans. What could it have been?" In the case of adolescence, it could be because early human society was much more complex than other animal societies, so we needed more time to learn the skills required.

### THEORY 2 – IT'S CULTURAL

There are adults who say, "Huh, it was different in my day. In my day we weren't *allowed* to feel like that. We just did what we were told. This modern teenage behaviour is all because there are not enough rules any more. If adults got tough and teenagers never watched television, there'd be no teenage behaviour to talk about." I would say these people are in denial. "Get real," I'd say. The Greek genius Aristotle talked about the strange behaviour of teenagers. And that was almost 2,500 years ago.

### THEORY 3 – IT'S THE NEED FOR INDEPENDENCE

All mammals need to leave their parents and set up on their own at some point. But human adults generally provide a comfortable existence – food arrives on the table in quantities, money is dished out at regular intervals and can be pleaded for more or less successfully, the bills get paid and the electricity for the TV doesn't usually run out. If teenagers didn't build up a fairly major disrespect for and irritation with their parents or carers, they'd never want to leave. In fact, falling out of love with the adults who look after you is probably a necessary part of growing up. Later, when you've gone, you can start to love them again because you won't need to be fighting to get away from them. And you can come back sometimes for a home-cooked meal and even bring your dirty washing with you if you play your cards right.

The need for separation could also explain why teenagers are far more concerned about what their friends think than what their parents think. Recent and ongoing research shows that teenagers even use different parts of the brain and sometimes make different decisions depending on whether their friends are with them. Friends are everything – because friends are what we need when we leave home. Humans rely on sociability. It makes sense to cultivate friends. In fact, this drive towards independence is possibly the most important thing about adolescence. It is, if you think about it, pretty much the whole point. And it's what your parents and all the adults who care about you want for you in the end. What they may not realise is that if you're going to be independent at 22 you may need to start rattling the bars of the cage at 14.

### THEORY 4 – IT'S JUST THE WAY THE BRAIN IS

We could simply say that it's not surprising the brain has this confusion and can't work entirely effectively, because there is so much change happening. Adolescence is an unfortunate side effect of all that change, and that's all there is to it.

Which theory do you find most interesting? Evolution? Culture? The struggle towards independence? Or just coincidence?

# Bedrooms – a mirror on
# the teenage brain

In the first edition of *Blame My Brain*, I was quite dismissive about untidy teenage bedrooms. I really didn't think they were important or interesting. Not my business, I thought. However, I have decided that perhaps they are quite interesting. (By the way, I know lots of teenagers don't have untidy bedrooms but let's face it: many do...) Here's what I think:

- Teenagers usually have a very small bedroom and a lot of stuff to keep in it. You also have to do a ridiculous number of things in your room so it's hardly surprising if it becomes a tip.

- You have far more important and stressful things going on in your lives than whether your bedroom is tidy or not.

- Many of you probably would like your bedroom to be tidy but the effort of tidying it is often greater than the desire for it to be tidy. A magic wand would be nice.

- An untidy bedroom is the result of dozens of tiny decisions: "Put it away now or drop it and put it away later." The first option is boring and unattractive, giving you an immediate unpleasant task (and you often focus more on the present, using your powerful emotional side.) The second option is easy, especially since the "putting it away later" bit feels very unreal and not worth thinking about, because it's not to do with the emotional pull of the present.

- It can be a wonderful way to annoy parents.

- It's actually quite a safe thing to argue about – better than smoking or alcohol or sex or homework or any of the other things that worry parents.

So perhaps your untidy bedroom (if you have one) could be a mirror of your mind: emotional, chaotic, rebellious and full of stress. Or maybe actually you really aren't bothered?

### What can you do about adolescence?

You might think you can't do anything about it, except go to sleep for a few years and wake up when it's all over. Actually, there's a lot you can do – not to stop it happening, but to deal with it and look at it differently.

- Enjoy it. Celebrate it. What is there to be negative about? Emotional reactions are good. In fact, you could say that without emotion we'd be pretty unsuccessful as a human race because we wouldn't be able to make any decisions. Logic on its own is not enough. Richard Cytowic, in *The Man Who Tasted Shapes*, talks about a wonderful fact from the animal kingdom: the Australian anteater has an extraordinarily large **frontal cortex**, much larger than the human one in comparison to the animal's size.[11] It should be well up there in the genius stakes. But, as you may have noticed, the Australian anteater has not exactly taken over the world; nor have Australian anteaters ever reached the moon or built cameras so small they can travel down a blood vessel. So what went wrong? Why are they so seemingly brainy but so conspicuously useless at anything apart from ant-eating? Well, rather interestingly, they have a very weak **limbic system** – the bit which is most important in emotions. They also apparently don't dream. Not even about ants. Australian anteaters are, perhaps, not nearly emotional enough. It's an interesting thought. Emotion may be very important indeed when it comes to success.

● Make the adults in your life read this book – they will soon see what's going on. They will sympathize and become immediately reasonable. Or, on second thoughts, don't let adults read this book – they will start being very smug, and make comments like:

"Never mind, you can't be expected to make a sensible decision because your teenage brain is in the middle of losing all its branches. Let me make the rules until you've grown up."

● Understand what is going on. Recognize that this is a necessary (and temporary) phase. Whatever anyone says or whatever you imagine they think, it does not mean you are a horrible person.

● Try to treat yourself and your brain kindly and with respect. Stress is a common part of adolescence – the stress hormone, **cortisol**, is more easily produced at this time. Some stress is good for us because it makes us do things, makes us able to perform well, but too much is not.

● Remember: although it's helpful and reassuring to know that this is all "normal", our brains develop and improve through *effort*. So (and I apologise for saying what you don't want to hear!) the more you *try* to make your brain behave in the way you want it to, the quicker it will. Exactly the same applies to adults, by the way. So, you have my permission to remind your parents, next time they do something wrong, that *they* may just need to try a bit harder. Don't blame me if that doesn't help, though. And please don't try it on your teachers.

What we now know about mirror neurons (see Brain Basic 2) also suggests that when you watch others exercising self-control (or doing whatever it is that you

---

### FASCINATING FACTS ABOUT YOUR ILLOGICAL, OVEREMOTIONAL BRAIN

- By the age of 6, the brain is 95% of its adult size, but during the teenage years the frontal cortex will increase and then decrease in thickness by perhaps 15–20% in some parts. The extra thickening comes mainly from increase in **dendrites** and synapses, and thicker axons. The thinning or pruning stage is important for good function.

- More neurons do not always mean a better brain. For example, in a condition called Fragile X, the problem is too many neurons. A good brain is well pruned and structured, with the pathways working effectively together.

- The gap which makes a synapse is very tiny: 200,000th of a millimetre. Roughly.

- Many studies show that a human frontal cortex is four

---

want to do better) it could help your brain develop in that way. So, the adults around you need to set a good example. We often learn by imitation.

times the size of a chimpanzee's. But some new ones suggest that they may be much more similar than that.
- The frontal cortex makes up 29% of the human brain but only 3.5% in cats – partly explaining why we are cleverer (though don't forget that bit about the Australian anteater).

Look what may happen when an adult has damage to the prefrontal cortex:
- loss of some social skills – has arguments, overreacts
- tendency to make inappropriate remarks
- difficulty grasping the moral of a story
- loss of ability to plan ahead or to work out what the result of an action will be

How many of those seem to affect many teenagers? Do any affect you? Maybe you could blame your brain and that not-quite-developed prefrontal cortex.

# TEST YOURSELF

## Can you read emotions in other people's faces?

Look at this picture of someone's eyes. Around the picture you will see four options.

Choose the one which you believe best describes what the person in the picture is thinking or feeling. Think about it carefully. Then do the same for all the pictures. Some of them are harder than others – don't worry if you find some difficult. It's important to choose something for every picture, though, so if you really can't decide, just make the best guess you can.

### Practice

jealous                           scared

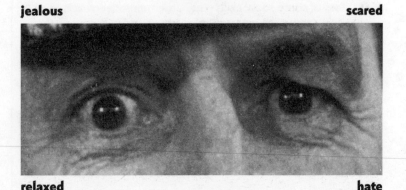

relaxed                         hate

**ANSWER: scared**

**1**

hate                                    surprised

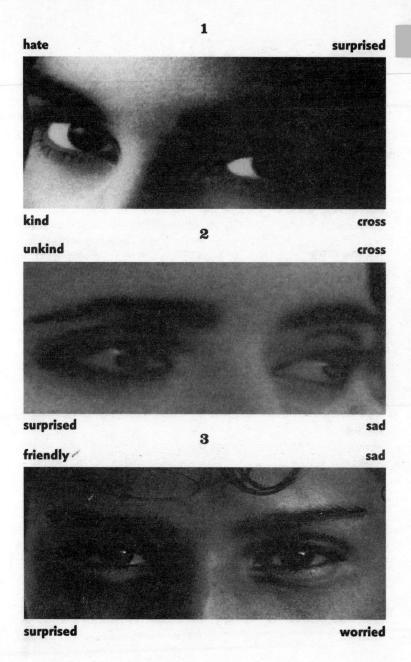

kind                                       cross

**2**

unkind                                     cross

surprised                                    sad

**3**

friendly                                     sad

surprised                                worried

**4**

relaxed                                          upset

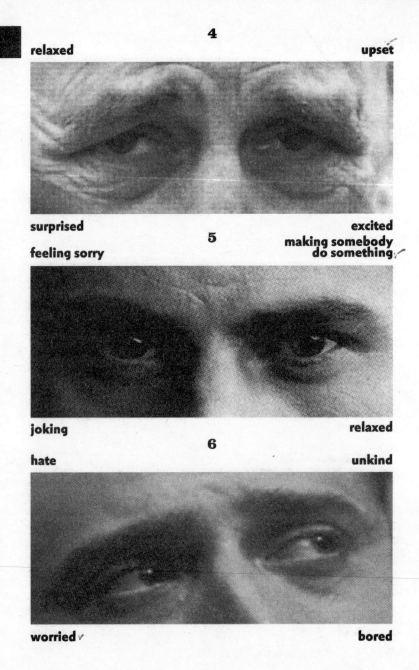

surprised                                        excited
**5**
feeling sorry                       making somebody
                                      do something

joking                                         relaxed
**6**
hate                                           unkind

worried ✓                                        bored

48

**7**

feeling sorry                    bored

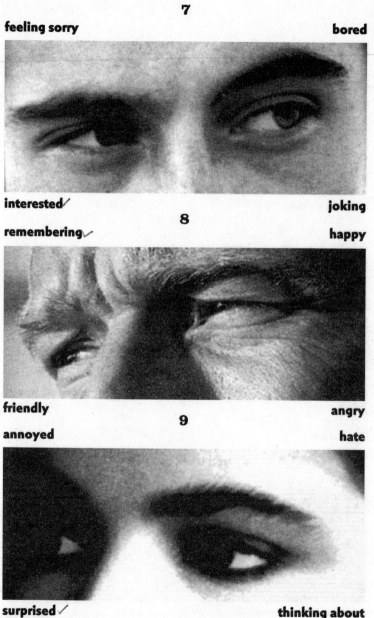

interested ✓                     joking

**8**

remembering ✓                    happy

friendly                         angry

**9**

annoyed                          hate

surprised ✓                      thinking about
                                 something

kind                                    ✓shy

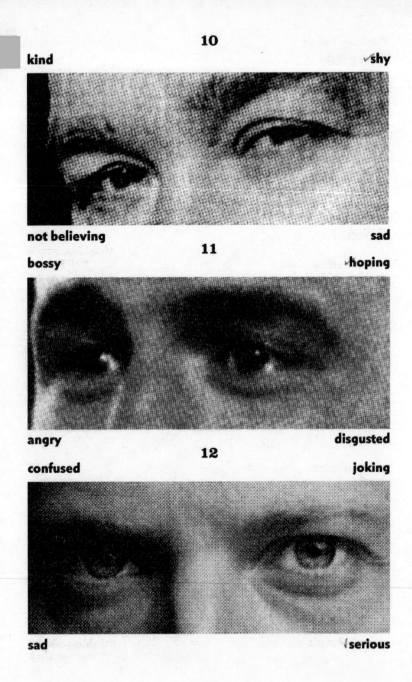

not believing                            sad

bossy                                ►hoping

angry                               disgusted

confused                              joking

sad                                 ✓serious

thinking about
something

**13**

✓upset

excited

happy

**14**

happy
thinking about
something

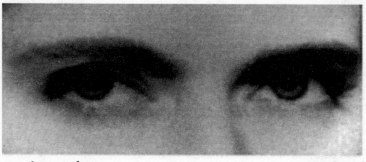

excited ✓

kind

not believing ✓

**15**

friendly

wanting to play

relaxed

51

**16**

made up her mind✓          joking

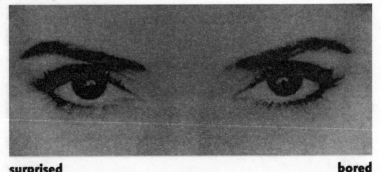

surprised          bored

**17**

angry          friendly

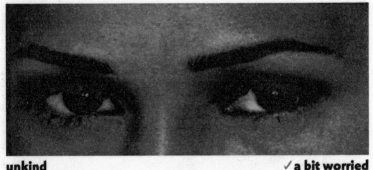

unkind          ✓a bit worried
thinking about
something sad✓

**18**

         angry

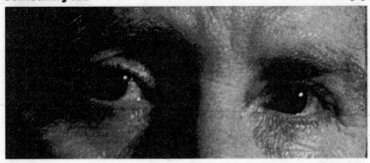

bossy          friendly

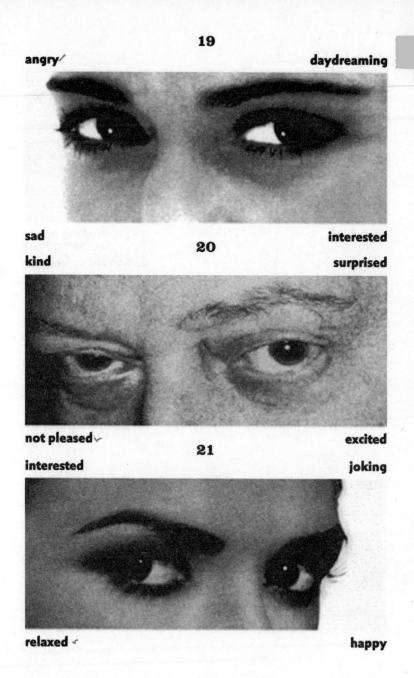

**19**

angry ✓                          daydreaming

sad                              interested

**20**

kind                             surprised

not pleased ✓                    excited

**21**

interested                       joking

relaxed ✓                        happy

53

**22**

playful                                                    kind

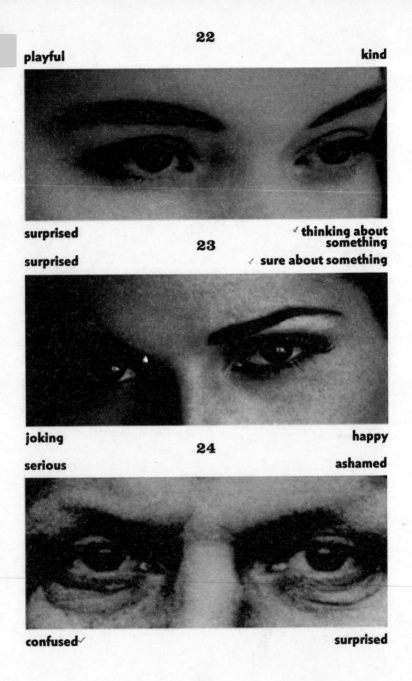

surprised                          ✓ thinking about
**23**                                  something
surprised                          ✓ sure about something

joking                                                     happy

**24**
serious                                                    ashamed

confused ✓                                                 surprised

**25**

shy                                                          ✓guilty

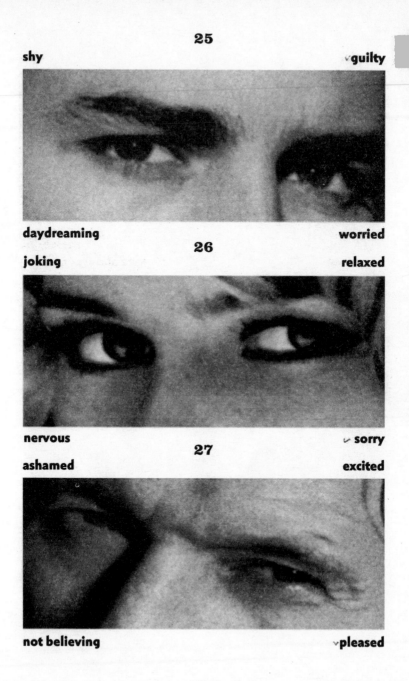

daydreaming                                                  worried

**26**

joking                                                       relaxed

nervous                                                      ✓ sorry

**27**

ashamed                                                      excited

not believing                                                ✓pleased

**disgust**  **hate**

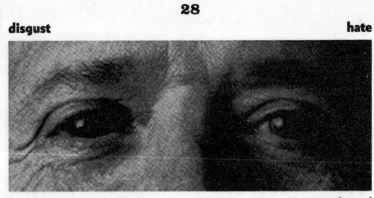

**happy**<sup>v</sup> **bored**

Now see how many you got right.

1   kind
2   sad
3   friendly
4   upset
5   making somebody do something
6   worried
7   interested
8   remembering
9   thinking about something
10  not believing
11  hoping
12  serious
13  thinking about something
14  thinking about something
15  not believing
16  made up her mind
17  a bit worried
18  thinking about something sad
19  interested
20  not pleased
21  interested
22  thinking about something
23  sure about something
24  serious
25  worried
26  nervous
27  not believing
28  happy

## WHAT DID YOU SCORE?

This test was designed for children up to the age of 12. There is also an adult version, which you can find in Simon Baron-Cohen's book *The Essential Difference* or on the Autism Research Centre website. They test the same things, and the pictures are the same, but the words used in the child version are easier and it is shorter. But the interesting thing is that no one has measured what would be normal results for teenagers. Why don't you get some of your friends to take this test and see if they score better or worse than 10–12 year-olds?!

The normal score for 10–12 year-olds is between 18 and 23. If you score over 23, you are very good at this test. If you score below 18, you are not so good at this skill. But if you are aged between 13 and 17 and scored poorly, maybe, just maybe, you are a victim of your changing teenage brain! It might be nothing to do with that, of course, but it's interesting to think about.

Acknowledgement: This test is called the "Reading the Mind in the Eyes" Test, "child version". It was first published in the *Journal of Developmental and Learning Disorders* (2001) in an article by Simon Baron-Cohen and others, and is reproduced with the kind permission of Simon Baron-Cohen at the Autism Research Centre at Cambridge University.

# CHAPTER TWO

# Sleep – And Lots of It

*"You can't expect me to get up for school – I didn't go to bed till two in the morning."*

*Meet Sam, the teenager who can't get out of bed.*

Sam can't get out of bed in the morning. Her dad stumbles into her room in his boxer shorts to wake her up. For the second time that morning. Her dad is disgusting; he smells of men's sweat and his legs are white and hairy, and Sam hasn't a clue how her mother can spend a night in the same bed as him. Fathers can be OK – from a distance, when they've showered, and only ever fully clothed. And when they have their wallets handy.

Sam didn't hear her dad come into her room ten minutes ago. She didn't hear him shout that she was going to be late for school, even though he distinctly heard a reply. Her brain did that automatically. Her younger brother is already dressed and is down in the kitchen feeding cereal to the dog. Her younger brother is disgusting too. He is twelve, spits, eats with his mouth open, leans over and breathes on her when she's on the computer, puts his stinking feet on the sofa when she's watching TV, picks his scabs and does a revolting sniff where you can hear the snot going down his throat.

Sam's brain knows perfectly well that this is not actually the morning – it's the middle of the night. She didn't go to bed till nearly two and it's now only five hours later. That's not a night's sleep, by any standards, and therefore this is NOT morning.

She falls asleep again. She doesn't mean to. Someone shakes her shoulder. She groans. It's her mum, grey-faced and fatty-eyed. What? Why is she being dragged out of bed now? Where is she? Who is she? *Why* is she?

"Are you awake, Sam?"

"Urrrhh."

"Get up now or you'll be late."

"Yurrrrh."

"Sam, do you promise you're getting up? I won't leave the room till you've promised."

"Yurrrh. Promsh."

Her mum leaves and Sam struggles to keep her eyes open. She stares at her clock, trying to make sense of it. Why did her mum wake her? She's got another five minutes till she has to get up. She closes her eyes.

Only a second later – but really twenty minutes later – she has two parents shouting at her that she's going to be late. She forces her eyes open, looks at the clock.

"Why the HELL didn't someone wake me up?"

Of course, Sam is tired all day at school. She can't concentrate in maths, hates physics anyway, drifts off in history and misses the homework instructions, perks up at lunchtime, almost falls asleep in French. She can only stare crossly at the teachers – their voices needle her brain and they wouldn't care how she was feeling even if she told them.

At three, Sam starts to feel wide awake. Just in time for the end of school. Back home, she fills herself with a sugary carbohydrate snack, rushes through her homework while watching television and settles down to a night of entertainment and organizing her social life.

The family meal is a temporary distraction, a mere interval to fuel her energy for the next few hours. The grumpier and more silent she is during the meal, the quicker they will let her go. And if she crashes the plates and perhaps even chips one while drying it, they'll soon snap at her to leave the dishes alone. Then she can retreat to the haven of her bedroom with its closed curtains and its gloomy cave-like quality.

During the evening, Sam's brain is spinning with energy and brilliance – she finalizes the complex plans for the school's Amnesty disco, which she is organizing, has the concentration and passion to write a two-page letter to a magazine complaining eloquently about the government's stance on Third World debt, and still has the time for a late-night philosophical phone discussion with her friend on the subject of the rights and wrongs of Mrs Legless's homework task.

When her family goes to bed, and her mum shouts at her to turn her music down, Sam puts on her headphones and turns the music up. She's been told it'll damage her ears, but that's just the sort of thing an adult would say to spoil her fun. Adults are full of scientific reasons why you shouldn't do things. Meanwhile, life's for living, the night is young and her TV is saying, "Let me entertain you" – which it does, until she begins to feel that she could just possibly go to sleep now. If she tried.

It's half past one in the morning.

## What's going on in Sam's brain?

For a long time, people have assumed that this inability to get out of bed is just teenagers being lazy. We have blamed it on the fact that they choose to stay up too late and therefore can't get up in the morning. But current research shows that laziness and deliberately late nights are not entirely to blame. It's the special teenage brain kicking in.

Circadian rhythms are the patterns of sleeping and waking, which all animals have. The brain region which seems most important in controlling these rhythms is deep within a part of the brain called the hypothalamus. We call the cells that control our waking patterns the biological or body clock.

In a normal and fully developed adult human brain, the body clock is "on" for about 16 hours a day, generally corresponding to daylight, and during this time we tend to be awake. In fact, it is quite difficult to sleep while the brain is like that.

Then the body clock switches off, usually responding to daylight disappearing, for around 8 hours, and we tend to feel sleepy during that time. In fact, it is hard to stay awake, unless we have a sleep problem or have something keeping us awake, like caffeine, or a party, or worry.

With younger children the pattern is different, depending on

**at 6 months**

**at 10 years**

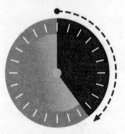

**at 15 years**

**as an adult**

age, with babies obviously sleeping for much longer. But it's worth noting that children of 9 and 10 tend to have reached the adult pattern of needing about 8 hours of sleep, though they do often sleep longer when undisturbed.

But teenagers are much more interesting than that, of course. Suddenly, around puberty, the body clock seems to work differently. Research shows that teenagers (and this is true until the early 20s) need around 9¼ hours of sleep a night.[12] You don't need to be a maths genius to work out that if you don't go to sleep till midnight, you are a long way from being ready to wake up when your parents attempt to rouse you at seven. Your body won't be ready till past nine.

Mmm, lie-in!

# Melatonin

When the body clock switches off, it tells our bodies to start feeling sleepy, and the brain produces a hormone called **melatonin**. This chemical prepares our brains to be sleepy. Tests have shown that in adolescence, melatonin is produced in the body much later in the evening than in younger children.[13] About the same as for adults, in fact. This is why you often don't feel sleepy until late in the evening. For teenagers, melatonin usually starts to increase around eleven at night (though levels are different depending how far into puberty you are). This doesn't mean that at eleven o'clock you suddenly fall over and sleep soundly on the kitchen floor: you still have to get to bed and do all that boring stuff with teeth, cleanser, spot cream and so on. You'll be much too tired to tidy your room, though, so don't worry about that.

By being forced to get up after only 7 hours instead of 9, you are building up a sleep loss of 10 hours during every school week. According to sleep expert Mary Carskadon, teenagers are getting on average 7$\frac{1}{2}$ hours of sleep on school nights. And a quarter are only getting 6$\frac{1}{2}$.

# REM sleep

Another problem with being woken too early is that you'll also be losing a special sort of sleep – **REM sleep**. REM stands for "rapid eye movement" because when you are in it your eyelids will be fluttering. REM sleep tends to happen at certain stages during your sleep cycle and is a particularly deep sleep. It is during this time that you dream. Experts now believe that REM sleep is particularly important for memory and learning.[14]

## SYMPTOMS OF LACK OF REM SLEEP INCLUDE

anxiety

depression

poor immunity

accidents

poor judgement

poor memory

hypersexuality (having too much sex drive)

slower reactions

Hormones for growth and sexual maturity are released mainly during sleep – so too little sleep could mean too few of the right hormones.

The stress hormone, cortisol, increases in sleep-deprived humans – less sleep means more stress.

So? Can't you just lie in at the weekend? Isn't that what weekends are for?

Unfortunately, life is not so simple. Although you can make up some sleep at weekends, this doesn't help your body clock and may actually disrupt it further. There is no doubt that, even with extra sleep at the weekends, very many adolescents show symptoms of severe sleep deprivation.

*Here are some scary statistics:*

- Sleep affects your grades: in a survey of sleep habits of 3,000 Rhode Island teenagers, those with the most sleep got As and Bs; those with the least got Cs and Ds.

- Sleep is strongly linked to mental health: one major study has shown that sleep-deprived people are 40 times more likely to suffer clinical depression.

- In a National Sleep Foundation study in the US, 24% of young adults of driving age said they had dozed off while driving.[15]

- Rats die faster when deprived of sleep than when deprived of food. The first sign that a sleep-deprived rat is dying is that it develops sores on its tail.[16]

## The sleeping teenage brain is really working very hard

There is evidence that your brain does a lot of its important development while you are asleep. It sounds like a wonderful new excuse for not handing in your homework: "Well, Mr Bumble, sir, you see, I read this book where it said my brain does a whole load of really important work while I am asleep so I thought you'd be really pleased about this, and so, well, I went to sleep. But guess what? When I woke up, the piece of paper I'd left by my bed was still completely blank."

Unfortunately, it's not quite as simple as that, but the truth is almost equally amazing. First, remember what happens in your brain when you do something or learn something, or even try to do something. (Look back at Brain Basic 2 if you need to.)

Remember that it's not the number of neurons you have that is important – it's the number of connections, and how strong those connections are. And the more times you do the same thing, or have the same thought, or recognize the same face, or understand the same piece of algebra (or even try to understand it), the more the connections between the relevant neurons increase and strengthen. This means that the next time you do it, it's a bit easier.

But the really amazing thing is that there is evidence that your sleeping brain practises the things you did while you were awake. In one study, scientists examined the brains of kittens whose brains were not yet fully developed.[17] They found that the connections between neurons in the brain physically changed during sleep, depending on what activity the kitten did during the day. Scientists can actually look at the kitten's brain and see a difference in the number and complexity of dendrites and synapses after sleep which follows a particular activity. Similar experiments have been done on rats.

If this also happens in human brains (and brain biology often seems to follow similar patterns in other mammals), this means that if you learn your history dates one evening, your brain could be rehearsing them, strengthening those connections, while you are in REM sleep, and you will do well in the test the next day. On the other hand, if you don't get enough REM sleep, this may not happen. Also, if you spend the evening slobbing out in front of some crummy piece of reality TV, the only thing your brain will find to practise during the night will be images of people shouting at each other or walking around with bare feet making inane remarks about nothing in particular.

All this brain activity happens for adults and younger children too, but there's something which makes teen-agers' brains different and is a reason why this is especially important for teenagers. It goes back to something I talked about in Chapter One: one of the most defining and fascinating things about teenagers' brains is that, contrary to what scientists used to believe, it is this time in your life when your brain is doing its most radical and fundamental changing since you were 2 years old.

Scientists call this "plasticity". It means that your brain is changing physically, growing new abilities in new areas. And what happens to your brain as it changes can have long-term effects on how it works.

So, the scary bit is that what you do to your brain in your teenage years is very important – much more important than was realized when your parents were teenagers. And one of the best things you can do is sleep – but sleep at the right time.

That, of course, is the problem. You can't change the time school starts in the morning (though some schools in the US have done this, with some success). You can't change your circadian rhythms. You can't radically change the time your brain decides to start producing melatonin.

But there are things you can do to get the most out of your body clock and to get the best sleep you can. I will suggest them at the end of this chapter.

## Why Might the Teenage Brain be Like This?

If you want to think about why the teenage brain is like this, here are some interesting theories. Remember, though, that they are not separate theories, just different ways of considering the issue, and they are all linked.

### THEORY 1 – IT'S EVOLUTION (1)

At some point in distant human prehistory, it may have been important for group survival that the newly strong adolescents were awake later into the night, so they could help adults protect the group. It's not important now, of course, but evolutionary biology takes many thousands of years to catch up. This theory doesn't, however, quite explain about wanting to sleep till noon – is it possible that there could ALSO be a smidgen of laziness involved here...?

### THEORY 2 – IT'S EVOLUTION (2)

Humans have an unusually long adolescence because the human adult's life is highly complex and the adolescent therefore has more to learn and more need to develop than other animals. Since we know that sleep is essential to brain growth and development, and since human adolescents have more developing to do, this would explain why teenage brains need more sleep.

### THEORY 3 – IT'S MAINLY CULTURAL

According to this theory, the reason teenagers don't go to sleep early enough and are therefore tired in the morning is that they are too busy in the evenings, exciting their brains with music, television, chat, family arguments and, occasionally, homework, so they simply aren't ready or willing to be sleepy till too late. Teenagers start to feel awake at 3p.m. because that's when school is about to end and life starts to get interesting.

### THEORY 4 – IT'S NATURE'S WAY

Sleep helps brain development and body growth. Teenagers' brains are developing enormously and their bodies are also suddenly growing: therefore they need more sleep.

It's likely to be a combination of these theories, of course. Nevertheless, there is no doubt, from studies on humans and other animals, that sleep patterns change in adolescence, and this can be measured by testing the amount of melatonin in the saliva at different times of the day.[18] Often teenagers are still producing melatonin mid-morning. Not surprising they're sleepy.

## How to make the most of your sleep patterns

Even though you can't stop having a teenage brain – and why would you want to? – there are things you can do to help yourself get the sleep you need when you need. You can minimize the effects of the sleep deprivation that the modern world forces on you. You still won't find that your brain does your history homework in your sleep, but you might even find you have the energy to do it yourself.

- Bright light in the morning is the best way to tell your body clock to wake up. It may sound unpleasant, but if someone opens your curtains and switches on all the lights before you need to get up, this will help.

- From lunchtime onwards, avoid coffee, tea, Coke with caffeine in (choose caffeine-free drinks) and tobacco (avoid tobacco altogether, in fact – but you know that).

- If you are sleepy during certain times of the day, try to use those moments for active, stimulating things so you avoid falling asleep, therefore keeping your body clock on cue for sleeping at night.

- Do try to catch up at weekends – by trying to go to sleep at a sensible time on at least one of the nights, rather than by sleeping in till lunchtime, which will not help your body clock.

- Try to help your body clock by getting lots of light through the morning and darkness in the evening. During the day, the more you can be outside, the more natural light you will get, helping your body clock.

- If getting to sleep is your problem, it is even more important not to compensate by sleeping late in the morning. Practise sleep hygiene (see the section below).

- A warm milky drink (not coffee or tea) can help – when milk is heated it contains a chemical which is a natural sleep inducer.

- Do not take sleeping pills to help you sleep unless a doctor prescribes them. There is nothing wrong with taking a mild herbal remedy sometimes, though you might start to think that you can't do without it, which is psychologically a bad idea. Ask your pharmacist for advice about what to choose. Contrary to popular belief, alcohol does not help you sleep.

- Lots of people find that lavender oil sprinkled on the pillow can help.

- I'm afraid you won't like this one but there's evidence[19] that when parents set a bedtime, teenagers do get more sleep and function better next day. (And when the bedtime was set at midnight, the study showed more instances of depression than when bedtime was set at 10pm. I did say you wouldn't like it!)

# Sleep hygiene

This is all about how to train your body to start thinking about sleep during the evening so you can fall asleep quickly. For an hour before your desired bedtime, follow these rules:

- Avoid excitement, computer games, arguments, anything difficult, loud/bright/thrilling television programmes, bright lights.
- Completely avoid alcohol – while you might think it makes you sleepy, it actually disrupts sleep patterns.
- Focus on relaxing: listen to music, potter around your room (yes, you could even tidy it, as long as you do this slowly and in a relaxed fashion).
- Gentle exercises, such as yoga or stretching, can be a good idea – but nothing that raises your heart rate or speeds up your breathing.
- Having a warm bath as part of your bedtime routine is another very good idea. Do it just before you go to bed. Putting lavender in your bath could help too.
- Stick to the same bedtime routine, so that your brain starts to link getting undressed and doing your teeth with going to sleep; personally, I find that writing my diary sends me to sleep – but that could be my boring life.
- When in bed, read or listen to quiet music for a short while, then turn the light off.

- Do not go online and do switch your phone off. Backlit screens are likely to keep you awake, as is the stress of someone contacting you.
- Don't spend more than 10–15 minutes trying to go to sleep. Just get up and read or potter about till you feel sleepy. Your brain has to learn that bed means sleep.
- Don't panic about how tired you will be in the morning – you'll be fine! A few bad nights will make no difference and you can catch up.

## Exam time

The hard fact is that if you are sleep-deprived you will not do your best in exams and tests (though sleeping badly for a few nights, as I have said, won't make enough difference). So, even if you follow none of the previous advice during the rest of the time, DO IT NOW.

A study at Harvard University in 2000 showed that during REM sleep the brain stores and rehearses recently learnt information.[20] So revising the evening before is good, but all-night cramming actually disrupts memory because you'll lose REM sleep.

## SOME SERIOUSLY SLEEPY STATISTICS

- 84% of US high-school children said they'd fallen asleep at school during the year (National Sleep Foundation's poll in 2000).

- About 50% of teenagers in a sample studied by US sleep expert Mary Carskadon showed symptoms of major sleep disorder.

- 60% of young adults admit to having driven while drowsy.

- A study in North Carolina found that in all the car crashes caused by falling asleep, more than half were caused by drivers aged 25 and younger.

- When schools have tried later start times, there have been benefits in health, behaviour, grades and statistics for car-crashes amongst school-age drivers.[21]

# TEST YOURSELF

## How sleepy are you?

Here is a short quiz to see how sleepy you are. It is used by doctors, but they use it as part of a range of other tests, so these results on their own are not enough to decide whether you have a real sleep problem.

Read each situation and decide how likely you usually are to fall asleep in that situation.

 **circle:**

| | |
|---|---|
| **0** | **no chance of falling asleep** |
| **1** | **slight chance** |
| **2** | **moderate chance** |
| **3** | **high chance** |

### SITUATION

*sitting and reading*

**0    1    2    3**

*watching TV*

**0    1    2    3**

*sitting still in a public place (e.g. cinema)*

**0    1    2    3**

*as a passenger in a car for an hour without a break*

**0     1     2     3**

*if you were to lie down for a rest in the afternoon*

**0     1     2     3**

*sitting and talking to someone*

**0     1     2     3**

*sitting quietly after lunch (e.g. in a lesson, or reading)*

**0     1     2     3**

*in a car, while stopped for a few minutes in traffic*

**0     1     2     3**

## SCORING – ADD UP YOUR SCORES

| | |
|---|---|
| **up to 9** | *average amount of sleepiness* |
| **10–13** | *mild amount of sleepiness* |
| **14–19** | *moderate amount of sleepiness* |
| **20–24** | *severe amount of sleepiness* |

For anything more than an average amount of sleepiness, you should consider that perhaps you are not getting enough sleep. Try some of the tips earlier in the chapter. If your sleepiness is causing problems for you, do see a doctor.

Acknowledgement: This test is the Epworth Sleepiness Scale, developed by Dr Murray W. Johns of the University of Melbourne, Australia. It is reproduced here with his kind permission (© M. W. Johns 1991–7). The wording has been very slightly changed for a teenage age range.

# CHAPTER THREE

# Taking Risks

"Why did I climb onto the school roof
and tie a bra to the flagpole?
Because I felt like it, that's all."

*Meet Marco. His parents have begun to dread
the phone ringing.*

It's the middle of Saturday night. Marco's parents are in bed. His father is asleep. His mother was asleep but she's wide awake now, aware that Marco has not come back. He is supposed to wake them to say he has returned. Her clock says one thirty. He was supposed to be home by one. Half an hour is not too bad. She's known worse. Much worse.

There was the time when the police brought him back. Drunk in charge of a supermarket trolley.

There was another time when the police brought him back. He'd been caught trying to attach a condom to the exhaust of a parked police car.

There was another time when the police brought him back. He was claiming not to know who he was. Turned out this was a dare. He was threatened with being charged with wasting police time for that one.

"What about wasting parents' time?" his dad asked. "What's the punishment for that?"

And it wasn't only Saturday nights they had to worry about. There was school. Four detentions so far that term. One of them for not turning up for a detention. One for smoking. Another one for climbing out of a classroom window during a lesson. And the other one for pretending he had just seen a vision of Jesus in the middle of a PE lesson. The last two were both dares, of course.

Not only detentions, either. Letters home. "Dear Mr and Mrs Fusilli, I have to bring to your attention the constantly disruptive behaviour of Marco in Mrs Doolally's sculpture lessons. Today he made a series of objects in the shape of body parts."

And the school reports: "Marco is a bright boy. However, his behaviour in class leaves a great deal to be desired. Marco seems to think his mission in life is to disrupt all his classes by clowning around." Or: "Marco undoubtedly has a great deal of talent. However, he goes to such enormous lengths to hide it that I am at a loss to know exactly what it is." Or the most recent one: "Marco will undoubtedly go far. However, this may not be entirely in the right direction."

Then there were the phone calls. "Cathy, I don't want to worry you but I'm sure I just saw Marco in the shopping centre during school hours. On Rollerblades. I suppose it might not have been him – he was moving very fast and he also seemed to be wearing a police helmet." Or: "Cathy, I don't want to worry you, but I'm sure that was Marco I nearly ran over just now. Walking across the main road with a blindfold on. Isn't it called chicken or something?" Or: "Mum, don't freak but I'm at the hospital. No, only my head."

And it wasn't just because he was a teenager. This had been going on since the day toddler Marco discovered that cutting the hair of his sister's Barbies produced a reaction of ear-splitting decibels. It continued at nursery when he dressed up as Superman and wanted to see if he could fly, so he leapt off a baby's high chair. While the baby was in it. It got worse at primary school, when he loosened the screws of Wally Frank's chair and Wally Frank crashed to the ground and challenged Marco to a fight to the death and bore a grudge against him for years, until Marco earned Wally Frank's respect by holding the flame of a cigarette lighter against his arm for ten seconds without making a sound. And in secondary school, this complete inability to do the quiet, sensible, career-improving thing extended to frequently being caught smoking even though he secretly hated it, deliberately setting off the fire alarm when a distinguished visitor was visiting the school, and never ever *ever* coming back on time from a night out.

So it is hardly surprising that his mum is lying awake, teetering halfway between terror and fury. Where is he? What is he doing? What sort of trouble is he in this time? Doesn't he understand how worried she gets? Doesn't he care about anyone?

She's had enough. She flings back the covers, stumbles downstairs and picks up the phone. With thick fingers and bleary eyes she punches in his mobile number. It rings. And rings. She is just about to give up when he answers.

His voice is blurred, his tongue fuzzy. For crying out loud, he's drunk again!

"Where the hell are you, Marco?" she hisses, trying not to wake the rest of the household.

"In bed. You just woke me up."

## What's going on in Marco's brain?

Marco is a risk-taker. Some people are and some people aren't, whether or not they are teenagers. If you are not a big risk-taker, you may sail through your teenage years without giving your parents a heart attack, though you may find plenty of other ways to raise their stress levels. If you have a risk-taking nature, there are some reasons why you will be likely to take this to extremes as a teen-ager. I'll come to those reasons in a minute.

But first, think about risk. Actually, we are all risk-takers in some way. We have to take risks in order to go about our daily life. You take a risk as soon as you get out of bed. (Though you could also be at risk if you stay in bed – you might get a blood clot, or an aeroplane might fall on your house.)

To be successful, we need to take risks, as teenagers and adults: if you want a particular job, you may have to face a stressful interview. You may fail at it, but if you don't take the risk you will certainly not get the job. You may have to apply for a difficult training course or to a top university; again, there is the risk of failure, the risk of meeting new people, the risk of being poor while you study. If you want to visit another country, you have to take a small risk by travelling.

Risk is not only about danger – it is also about trying

something new, something we may not succeed at first time, or something we may not like. If we were programmed never to take any risks, we would never achieve anything, and the human race would have failed before it started. We would not eat the things we do, in case they were poisonous. We would not have hunted, built aeroplanes, travelled to other countries, met new people, found new ways of using our environment, or discovered anything.

It is the same in the animal kingdom: an antelope chooses to risk going for a patch of grass, even though there is a chance that a lion is watching, because eating that grass will make it stronger and fitter for survival. But does an antelope think like this, in terms of balancing risks? Almost certainly not. What actually happens is that antelopes and humans and other animals are biologically programmed to seek reward, or pleasure. The antelope knows that the patch of grass looks tasty; only on a deeper, unconscious survival level does it "know" that the patch of grass will give it greater strength and therefore mean that it will have a greater chance of passing on its genes to lots of baby antelopes (which is how animals define success). If it was just about risk and fear, the antelope would never go for the grass – but it's about desire for pleasure, and it is desire for pleasure that makes us act, risky or not. Survival and achievement are a delicate balance of risk and caution, spurred on by pleasure.

## Dopamine – the pleasure factor

Taking risks or, more accurately, *surviving* risks gives us pleasure. You know the feeling when your plane lands safely? If you have been on a roller coaster or any thrill ride, you'll know that feeling of ecstasy when the ride finishes and you are safe again. People scream during the ride – but look at their faces when they finish. Personally, I hate those rides, but I do remember loving the feeling of euphoria afterwards. That's the whole point of the word "thrill".

But this feeling of pleasure is not just to do with thinking, Wow, I survived that risk – how wonderful that I'll go on to live another day! There is also something physical going on in the brain which produces the pleasure. And this is the same for everyone, teenagers or not.

A brain chemical called **dopamine** activates these feelings of pleasure. It is a special chemical called a **neurotransmitter**. Neurotransmitters pass impulses between neurons. Dopamine has many functions but one is to do with pleasure. Not the sort of quiet pleasure you get from slobbing out with a bar of chocolate in front of the TV; dopamine is responsible for the much more dramatic feelings of pleasure – thrill and excitement. It puts the *wow!* factor into your life.

> **Dopamine's job is to make you want pleasure or reward.**
> **It makes you choose to take a particular action which will give**
> **you pleasure. The more your dopamine system is activated,**
> **the more you want pleasure, and the more likely you are**
> **to go looking for it.**

When researchers removed the dopamine system from rats, the rats stopped seeking out new things. We need this element of thrill-seeking, otherwise we become lazy.

Though we all want pleasure, some people's brains seem more geared up to looking for it than others. These people perhaps have a more active (sometimes overactive) dopamine system. What happens then is this: the more excitement you get, the more dopamine is released in your brain, and then the more excitement you want. You could say that you become hooked on excitement.

## What makes teenagers special when it comes to risk-taking?

If all humans are programmed to take some risks in order to succeed, and if some people (of all ages) enjoy more risks than others, what makes teenagers different? Many adolescents certainly do take more risks, and more dangerous ones. Nearly half the new cases of HIV in the UK occur in under 25s. Young drivers are four times more likely to die in car accidents, and young drivers are much more likely to speed, to drink and drive, and not to wear seat belts.

Many studies show interesting differences between adults and teenagers when it comes to dopamine: differences in levels and differences in how at least some adolescents react to the excitement of risk-taking or novelty-seeking. One interesting finding[22] is that the reward centre of the teenage brain may ignore a small reward but produce an exaggerated thrill reaction after a medium-sized excitement. This means that if you are a thrill-seeker, it could require a bigger risk to produce the desired thrill sensation. There's also a suggestion that a part of the brain called the **ventral striatum**, important in reacting to excitement, is less active in teenagers – or some teenagers. So, some of you may have to take more dangerous risks to get the amount of pleasure chemical your brains crave.

Even teenagers who are not particularly big risk-takers may suddenly take a risk which is out of character. This may be a desire to fit in or impress their friends – some experts say that the greatest risk-takers often have the lowest self-esteem. These teenagers may feel that taking risks is the best way to get people to respect, notice and like them. Or their uncharacteristic risk-taking could be simply a sudden lack of judgement. Or it may be that they didn't even see it as a risk – they just "felt like doing it".

This idea of "just feeling like it" is really important when we look at a teenage brain. It connects with the pleasure angle again – it is a gut reaction desire for pleasure. It seems that gut reaction is a stronger motivator for teenagers than thinking ahead. You *can* think ahead but you're less likely to base your decision on that than on emotion. And remember: to think ahead and weigh up risks logically requires a working prefrontal cortex.

Much research shows that teenagers base their decisions about risk more on how they feel now than on thinking ahead to what might happen. The part of our brain that we need to make good decisions based on judging consequences and risk is the prefrontal cortex. As you know, yours isn't fully developed yet, even if it's trying very hard (and sometimes fMRI scans show it working even harder than an adult one). You *can* perfectly well work out what the risks are but you may simply find it harder to base your decision on logical reasoning than on how you feel *now*. Research also suggests[23] that teenagers take a little longer to decide what is dangerous and what isn't.

One fascinating recent finding[24] is that teenagers also make different decisions *and have different brain activity* depending on whether their friends are present when they are deciding what risks to take. The need to impress friends is important for getting on in life and becoming independent of parents, but sometimes the risks taken can be more dangerous. Some statistics show that teenagers are far more likely to have a car accident or commit a crime when in a group than when alone.

## Why should teenagers be different in this way?

We can look at reasons for this from several angles. As before, they come down to the different ways in which we can look at human behaviour. And as before, the ideas are linked and evolution is at the root of why we are the way we are and why we behave the way we do.

### THEORY 1 – IT'S EVOLUTION

This idea says that teenagers originally became risk-takers because it gave us an advantage in early human times: as adolescents moved towards adulthood, when they would have to look after themselves and produce a family of their own, they could only learn to be bold and successful later by taking risks while still protected by their parents – in other words, in relative safety. It is all about learning what you can safely do and what you can't. It allows valuable mistakes. Also, in evolution, the stronger survive, and risk is strengthening – it may get you the better food, the stronger mate, the better environment.

\* \* \* \* \*

## THEORY 2 – IT'S BIOLOGICAL

This goes back to the theory that the prefrontal cortex is not developed and therefore can't make sensible decisions, can't think ahead to look at consequences and is incapable of reason. As you saw on page 45, someone with damage to this part of the brain can't make good judgements either and is likely to take great risks. According to this theory, the parent or adult is there to make the decisions until the teenager has developed this reason.

However, if this theory is true, why are many adults also risk-takers, leaping out of planes and running in front of stampeding bulls? In answer, I would say that the risks that some teenagers take are not based on calculated decisions – when Marco drank four vodkas and climbed into a shopping trolley, he had not even begun to measure risk. He "just felt like it".

He didn't think.

## THEORY 3 – ACTUALLY, TEENAGERS ARE BEING VERY RATIONAL

Teenagers take risks for a very good reason, though it may be subconscious: they want to be accepted, part of the group. This is a very important aspect of being human. Teenagers rightly want to establish their place in society, strengthen bonds with friends, assert their status.

* * * * *

Adolescent behaviour is triggered by the start of puberty. Puberty starts on average 2 years earlier in the developed world than it did 50 years ago. So teenage risk-taking begins earlier too, at a time when the brain is not ready to calculate and decide. Added to this, the possible risks nowadays are worse: drugs are stronger and more widely available; alcohol is more widely used; teenagers have more money and more access to riskier night-time activities such as clubbing; there is less taboo about sex; and teenagers are empowered to make more of their own choices and decisions. At the same time, teenagers are often restricted from many of the milder forms of risk-taking (such as riding a bike in the countryside and generally spending free time out and about without supervision), leaving only the more risky activities available, such as alcohol, drugs and sex.

## Another side of risk-taking

Negative risk-taking is not just about jumping into shopping trolleys or getting into trouble through high spirits. It can also be about unhealthy eating and not caring for your own body. That may not feel like risk, but it is.

In 2003 the British Medical Association called the teenage lifestyle a "potential public health time-bomb". According to that report, the three main risk factors are obesity, alcohol consumption and sexual activity. Some under 16s admit to drinking an average of ten units of alcohol a week; three fifths of 16–24 year-olds admit to not using condoms; rates of sexually transmitted diseases are rocketing; almost a quarter of 15-year-olds are regular smokers and a third have tried cannabis; a fifth of 15-year-olds are classified as obese. This means that adolescents are the only age group where health is getting worse.

Just as it's risky to eat too much, or too much junk food, it's also risky not to eat enough, or enough beneficial foods. Teenage girls are frequently on diets (60% at any one time) and often when they are not overweight. By not being careful about what you eat – or don't eat – at this age, you can miss out on the vitamins and minerals essential for your future health. That's a risk too.

Your parents will remember a Billy Joel song called "Only the Good Die Young". He was wrong. Risk-takers die young too.

## Alcohol

Alcohol needs its own section in a book on the teenage brain. We associate alcohol with pleasure. We also associate it with risk. Unfortunately, the special teenage brain does special things with alcohol, which multiplies the risk hugely. Scientists don't yet know all the reasons why, but the adolescent brain is exceptionally vulnerable to alcohol and other drugs.

One reason why alcohol has become a problem in recent years is that so many teenagers drink vodka. It is much easier to get very drunk on a spirit such as vodka than it is on wine or beer, and it's harder to know how much you've had. It's easy to disguise the taste with sweet drinks that slip down fast. I'm afraid the truth is that scientists say there is no safe limit of alcohol for teenagers. When adults who care about young people warn you of the dangers, we do so because we are genuinely worried, not because we want to spoil your fun. It is not fun to damage your brain. It really isn't.

You don't want to be told "Don't get drunk", and you'll probably take no notice if I say it. Unfortunately, however, thanks to our new knowledge of the teenage brain, it's a message we can't get away from. If you *are* going to drink, at least know what you are getting yourself into. Then ask yourself why you would abuse your brain in that way.

> For some reason, alcohol tends to make adults sleepy, but it does not have this effect on teenagers – it tends to make them hyper and more likely to do something stupid.[25]

*Here are some brutal truths:*

- A study at the University of California, San Diego, in 1999 found that teenagers who start drinking before 15 are
  1. 5 times more likely to become heavy drinkers as adults

2. 10 times more likely to be involved in a serious fight
3. 7 times more likely to be involved in a crash
4. 12 times more likely to be injured in an accident

- Studies in rats show that it takes only half the alcohol to damage an adolescent brain that it takes to damage an adult one.[26]

- This damage to the brain is likely not to recover. Although our brains are capable of *some* remodelling after injury, alcohol damages crucial parts involved in memory and learning and any repair would be extremely difficult, lucky or impossible.

- Teenagers who averaged two drinks a day for two years showed a 10% loss of performance on memory tasks (worse than adults with severe alcoholism).[27]

- In the 15–24 age group, half of accidental deaths involve alcohol or drugs; so do many suicides.

All the evidence shows that the teenage brain is horribly vulnerable both to the possibility of addiction and also to the immediate effect of alcohol itself. In addition, the liver can't process alcohol as well as an adult liver. Therefore a teenager takes less alcohol to get drunk, the effect is worse, and the brain never recovers from the onslaught.

Many areas of the brain that change most during adolescence seem sensitive to alcohol. In laboratory experiments, adolescent rats exposed to alcohol had noticeable damage to parts of the frontal cortex. In humans with alcoholism, the **hippocampus** is significantly smaller – this part is very important for memory. So, two of the brain parts that show most change in normal adolescence are the very ones which are most vulnerable to alcohol damage. Doctors are now seeing teenage patients with advanced and incurable alcoholic brain and liver diseases, which they used to see only in much older people.

Long-term alcohol use may lead to addiction and will certainly lead to permanent brain damage, but the problem doesn't stop there. It's not just about long-term drinking: it's about getting drunk. And you don't have to do it very often. One drinking binge does not make you an alcoholic. But it might kill you before you get the chance to be an alcoholic.

### THE DANGERS OF ALCOHOL

*There are many ways of dying or coming to great harm through one major encounter with alcohol:*

- you could inhale your own vomit
- you could drive a car
- you could get into a car driven by a drunk friend
- you could decide to walk home alone
- you could fall off the pavement into the path of a car
- you could be picked up by someone who wishes you harm

- you could be raped – and you might not even remember the next morning
- you could have sex and wish you hadn't
- and you could – no, you will – destroy brain cells, more brain cells than an adult would

*Another risk of being drunk is unwanted pregnancy:*
- 75% of 16–20 year-olds who have sex use contraception while sober; only 13% use contraception when drunk.
- One US study found that nearly a third of pregnant 14–21 year-olds had been drunk when they became pregnant.
- Another study found that 40% of 13–14 year-olds who had had sex were either drunk or on drugs when they had their first sexual experience.

"Oh, that won't happen to me," you say. "I would never do those things. I would never let alcohol make me lose control." That's because you are sober and in control while you are reading this. Alcohol takes away your control. Yes, it gives you pleasure – otherwise why would anyone drink? But your dopamine system kicks in, you want more pleasure, and more pleasure, and before you know it you are taking the biggest risk of your life. You've damaged your brain and it's the only brain you'll ever have.

# "Drugs — surely cannabis is ok?
# Isn't it so much safer than alcohol?"

"It's just a bit of weed." Well, maybe that's what cannabis or marijuana is made of, but it's a mind-altering drug. So is alcohol. So is heroin. People who say cannabis is safe are deluding themselves – and you. People believe what they want to believe, but even those who used to say it's safe are now having to face facts based on the latest research:

- Cannabis smoke contains high levels of chemicals which cause cancer – just like normal cigarettes.

- It damages memory, concentration and coordination.

- Using it over a long time puts you at greater risk of clinical depression and **schizophrenia** and one large long-term study in New Zealand has recently suggested that frequent use over many years may reduce IQ (a measure of intelligence).

- Side effects are panic attacks, nausea and hallucinations.

- It can be very hard to stop using cannabis – in other words, it can be addictive.

- It builds up in the body over time – unlike alcohol, which is eliminated by the liver.

- There is no recommended safe level, because no one knows what is safe where cannabis is concerned.

If alcohol is more dangerous for teenagers than for adults, cannabis will be, too. More and more studies show that cannabis has serious long-term dangers, including a risk of later mental illness. If you take drugs, you are taking huge risks, just as you are with alcohol.

Remember: Cannabis was recently downgraded to a class C drug. It is still illegal. You can still be arrested for possession, even for personal use. You can still go to prison for supplying or selling it to anyone.

## Cigarette smoking

Yes, yes, you know it's bad for you. You all know about lung cancer, heart disease, breathing problems. You probably ignore those things because they won't happen till you're older – your parents' age, perhaps.

And you won't become addicted, will you? Well, the truth is you are more likely to become addicted if you start now than if you wait a few years. In rats, nicotine is twice as addictive in adolescent rats as adult rats. There's also evidence that if your addiction starts early, it will be stronger later – you'll find it harder to give up. Unfortunately, that special teenage brain needs protecting from cigarettes too.

## "Help! I don't do any of these things. I must be boring!"

Actually, most teenagers don't.

- A quarter of UK teenagers get drunk at least three

times a month. That means three quarters don't.

- In a major study, 26% of girls aged 16–19 and 30% of boys of the same age admitted they'd had sex before the age of 16 – that means that 74% of girls and 70% of boys taking part had not.
- Drug-taking has decreased annually slightly among young people in England, between 2001 and 2011.
- The number of 11-15-year-olds in the UK who drank alcohol also decreased between 1988 and 2007, though those who did drink tended to drink more.
- The majority of teenagers do not get arrested, drunk, pregnant or killed. You are in the majority.

Taking risks is not about being brave. It's about judgements and decisions. Clever and sensible people act after weighing up results and working out whether the pain or risk is worth the resulting pleasure or success. Sometimes it isn't, so sometimes the risk should not be taken. You may think you are boring because you don't do the stuff that gets your friends into trouble, but there are plenty of other ways to be dynamic, bold and successful.

Sometimes saying no to something is just as risky and difficult, and requires just as much bravery. And if you don't do all this stuff, maybe it's because you matured early and your frontal cortex is extra clever and making all the right decisions already. You just escaped the experimental stage your friends are going through. You grew up faster.

## "Hey! I do all of these things.
## I'm so cool!"

Some risk, as we have seen, is necessary for your learning (and important for the human race in evolutionary terms, even if on an individual level it kills you). It also adds a bit of spice to life. There are lots of things which you probably say to yourself to justify the crazy things you do:

- everyone else does it
- you're only young once
- it (death/arrest/addiction) will never happen to me
- plenty of adults smoke/get drunk/take drugs/drive too fast
- it's a brilliant feeling

Those things are all very well, and natural. However, at some point common sense has got to kick in. At some point you have to take control of your life and recognize that there are consequences to your actions. The first consequence may be pleasure, but clever people look ahead to the next consequences as well.

## What Can You Do To Help Your
## Risk-Taking Teenage Brain?

- Make choices. Real choices, not things you are pushed into doing by your friends or the dizzy parts of your brain. You can get your dopamine fix in lots of other exciting ways: sport, roller coasters, skateboarding, go-karting and trampolining will all give you the same rush.

- Get into trouble if you must, but do it in a way that doesn't harm your future, your health, or someone else. Otherwise you may live to regret it. If you are lucky.
- Are you nearly 17? It seems that sensible decision-making improves from around the age of 17. You've survived this far – you're nearly out of danger. Well done!

**RISKY FACTS**

- Alcohol increases the dopamine in the brain, making the drinker more likely to seek pleasure and take risks.
- In a study, those classed as high risk-taking personalities were ten times more likely to take drugs than low risk-taking personalities.
- Nearly half of new HIV/Aids cases each year are in under 25s.
- Stress also affects dopamine levels and may make you take more risks.
- Food, alcohol, drugs and sex all increase dopamine levels: they are all things which humans seek out for pleasure. Food and sex are important for the survival of the human race – alcohol and drugs are not.
- 4% of UK 11–15 year-olds had used a class A drug in the previous year – 96% had NOT.
- Of 35 European countries, the UK has the third-highest figure for 15-year-olds saying they were drunk at least 10 times in the last year.[28]

There are lots of good resources and facts here:
On alcohol:
**www.drinkaware.co.uk/check-the-facts/alcohol-and-the-law/ the-law-on-alcohol-and-under-18s**
On drugs:
**http://teenadvice.about.com/od/drugfactsforteens/ Drug_Facts_for_Teens.html**

# TEST YOURSELF

## How much of a risk-taker are you?

Here is a short quiz to assess your desire to take risks and seek out thrills.

Read these pairs of statements and for each one circle **A** or **B** depending on which better describes the way you think or feel. If you disagree with both statements, just choose the one you least dislike. It is important to give an answer to each item. You must be honest about your feelings – this is not about right or wrong decisions but about what is true for you.

**1**  **A**  I like wild uninhibited parties.
   **B**  I prefer quiet parties with good conversation.

**2**  **A**  I dislike people who do or say things just to shock or upset others.
   **B**  When you can predict almost everything a person will do and say, he or she must be a bore.

**3**  **A**  I usually don't enjoy a film or a play where I can predict what will happen in advance.
   **B**  I don't mind watching a film or a play where I can predict what will happen in advance.

**4**  **A**  I would not like to try any drug which might produce strange or dangerous effects on me.

  **B**  I would one day like to try some of the drugs that produce hallucinations.

**5**  **A**  A sensible person avoids activities that are dangerous.

  **B**  I sometimes like to do things that are a little frightening.

**6**  **A**  I like to try new foods that I have never tasted before.

  **B**  I like eating the same things so I'm not disappointed.

**7**  **A**  I would like to try waterskiing.

  **B**  I would not like to try waterskiing.

**8**  **A**  I prefer down-to-earth kinds of people as friends.

  **B**  I would like to make friends in some of the "far-out" groups like artists or among people who dress in unusual ways.

**9**  **A**  I prefer the surface of the water to the depths.

  **B**  I would like to go scuba-diving.

**10** **A** I would like to try parachute-jumping.

  **B** I would never want to try jumping out of a plane, with or without a parachute.

**11** **A** I am not interested in experience just for the sake of it.

  **B** I like to have new and exciting experiences and sensations even if they are a little frightening, unusual or illegal.

**12** **A** For me, a good piece of art must be balanced and clear, and its colours must go well together.

  **B** I often enjoy the clashing colours and irregular forms of modern art.

**13** **A** I enjoy spending time in the familiar surroundings of home.

  **B** I get very restless and bored if I have to stay home for any length of time.

**14** **A** I like my boy/girlfriend to be physically exciting.

  **B** I like my boy/girlfriend to share my values and interests.

**15** **A** The worst sin when socializing with friends is to be rude.

**B** The worst sin when socializing with friends is to be boring.

**16** **A** A person should have wide sexual experience before marriage.
   **B** It's better if two married people begin their sexual experience with each other.

**17** **A** I like people who are sharp and witty, even if they do sometimes insult others.
   **B** I dislike people who have their fun at the expense of other people's feelings.

**18** **A** There is too much portrayal of sex in films.
   **B** I enjoy watching many of the "sexy" scenes in films.

**19** **A** People should dress according to some standard of taste, neatness and style.
   **B** People should dress in individual ways, even if the effects are sometimes a little strange.

**20** **A** Skiing down a mountain is a good way to end up on crutches.
   **B** I think I would enjoy the sensations of skiing very fast down a steep mountain.

Turn the page for your results.

# RESULTS

The test does not simply analyse one type of risk-taking. There are actually four things being tested. Let's take one at a time.

**THRILL AND ADVENTURE-SEEKING** – This measures how keen you are to do things that may be physically danger-ous, such as mountaineering. Scoring highly suggests that you enjoy some of the things we usually consider risky or dangerous.

*Score one thrill and adventure-seeking point for each of* **5B, 7A, 9B, 10A, 20B. Total ... out of 5**

**EXPERIENCE-SEEKING** – This measures how keen you are to experience new things and to be different from other people, perhaps following "different" rules. Scoring highly means you are keen for new experiences – even if a little risky – but not necessarily physically dangerous ones.

*Score one experience-seeking point for each of* **4B, 6A, 8B, 12B, 19B. Total ... out of 5**

**DISINHIBITION** – This measures how important you feel it is not to have inhibitions in social situations, like parties. An inhibition is something inside you that stops you doing something that might be fun, because you think it is wrong or too risky. Scoring highly suggests that you like to lose your inhibitions in social situations and perhaps that you like to "let yourself go".

*Score one disinhibition point for each of **1A, 11B, 14A, 16A, 18B. Total ... out of 5***

**BOREDOM SUSCEPTIBILITY** – This measures how easily bored you become by either repeated experiences or predictable people. Scoring highly means you are easily bored.

*Score one boredom susceptibility point for each of **2B, 3A, 13B, 15B, 17A. Total ... out of 5***

You can also add up all your scores together, to give you a general picture of how comfortable you are with risk in general. How do you compare with your friends?

Acknowledgement: This test is from the Sensation Seeking Scale (SSS-V).
It was originated by Dr Marvin Zuckerman of the University of Delaware.
His original test has 40 questions. It is reproduced and shortened here with
his kind permission. I have slightly changed the wording
of some questions to adapt it for teenagers.

# CHAPTER FOUR

# Girls and Boys – Different Bodies, Different Brains?

*"Size is not what counts – it's what you do with it."*

*Meet this group of fifteen-year-olds in their lunch break. It's the first day back after the Christmas holidays, so it's a time for comparing new possessions, radical hairstyles and the stories of what they did – or didn't – get up to during the holidays. And there's a new girl too...*

"Hey, Sanjay!"

"Hey, Johnno!" Sanjay slaps Johnno on the back and tips his schoolbag upside down. Johnno dives at the bag and grabs it just as the contents are about to fall out, skilfully and simultaneously lashing out with his foot at Sanjay, who swerves and leaps onto a chair.

"Hey, Sanjay!" shouts someone else.

"Hey, Leroy!" reply Sanjay and Johnno together.

"You seen Tommo's new phone?" says Leroy, who has just come into the room with Tommo.

"Nah, cool! Gissa look, Tommo," shouts Johnno.

Tommo has head-phones on. He doesn't hear the others talking to him as he walks past. Johnno throws his bag at Tommo's legs and Sanjay tackles him from behind.

"Hey, what you doin'?" exclaims Tommo.

"Show 'em your phone," says Leroy.

"Yeah, what's the spec?" asks Sanjay.

"64GB Hard drive."

"Weight?"

"One hundred and thirty-two grams."

"Cool. Looks thin too."

"Eight point four millimetres – you don't want it too thin, imo."

"Camera spec?"

"Two cameras – main one is eight Mega pixel and an HD video at 30 frames per second."

"Cool screen."

"Yeah, it's 4.8inch at HD, and backlight for clear visibility in low-light conditions. The whole device is packed with features – here, you want to see the list?"

"Does it come in different colours?"

The boys turn their heads to see who has spoken. A girl. Cherry. She is with a group of other girls. They are all looking over to the boys. And laughing. One of them has her legs draped over another girl's lap. One is applying lipstick to another's lips. They all sit close together. Touch one another often.

"What?" asks Tommo.

"Does it come in different colours?"

111

"I dunno. What if it does?"

Another girl, Lara, speaks. "Yeah, it does. I've got one actually. Blue. A really deep turquoise blue. Like a tropical beach in a holiday brochure. Reminds me of Barbados. You can get it in cerise too."

Tommo shouts over, "So, you got one too? What, in the same model? You got the 64 gig, too?"

Lara rolls her eyes. "God, I don't know. Great for texting and fits in my PE skirt pocket without Stalin seeing it – that's all I need to know. And it was on a really cheap contract – special deal from that new shop. Which is important when your olds are as tight-fisted as mine. Frugal times call for frugal measures."

Sanjay is interested. "Hey, where's the shop, man? Lead me to it."

"That shop on the street that goes down behind the library? Can't remember the name of the shop. Red writing, I think. Maybe with black?"

"I dunno what you're talking about. Wexford's?"

"No. You know the coffee shop where we once saw Mr Peccadillo with Miss Beard? Well, just near there, there's a street that looks all old-fashioned and atmospheric. Well, not that street but a few more streets down, maybe three – I'd know it if I saw it – well, down that street there's a chemist's, then a baker's, then a shop with a blue door, then a shop with a red door. Well, it's either that one or the one next

112

to it. Come on, YOU know."

"I know where she means," says Tommo. "Best to come from the other direction, from school. Start from the east end of Main Street, go north fifty metres, turn right into Jewel Street and there's a shop about seventy-five metres along on your left. That's it."

But no one is listening. The door has opened, which Tommo couldn't see at first because it's behind him. Caroline has come in. With a girl they've never seen before. Tall, blonde, drop-dead, and so on. And legs. Legs that presumably do end somewhere and Tommo desperately tries not to think about where. Not now – now is absolutely not the time.

Everyone looks at her. Caroline leads her over to the girls.

"Hey guys, this is Sasha. She's just started here today, poor girl. Sasha, this is Cherry, Lara, Aisha, George – short for Georgina – and that's Sarah with the seriously wicked hair. Oh, and those are obviously the boys over there. Say hello to Sasha, boys."

"Hello, Sasha," they croak. All of them want to say something but nothing seems to come out. Sanjay gets out his phone instead and Johnno starts rummaging in his bag.

Finally, Leroy manages to speak. "Hey, Sasha. Come and see Tommo's new phone."

Sasha walks over. She towers over them and they

wish they were standing instead of slouched on vinyl chairs covered in chewing gum. Her legs really do go on ... for ever.

Tommo holds out his phone for her to look at. The boys all nudge each other. They still can't think what to say but if they laugh enough it won't matter.

"It comes in different colours," says Tommo. "Like blue and, I dunno, what did Lara say?"

"Cerise," says Johnno.

"Yeah, cerise," continues Tommo. "You might like that. Suits your..." He is going to say "eyes" but suddenly he thinks, Christ, what colour is cerise anyway? Maybe that's not an eye sort of colour. He says nothing, his tongue tangled somewhere between a word and a hard place.

Sasha hands it back to him. "Yeah, it's nice," she says. "Not bad for a toy. I had that before I got the new X4. I just find I value the faster shutter speed at forty per second, advanced Bluetooth technology using the new protocols, and G4 as standard. What with that and the fact I can add in an extra 32GB memory with a Micro SD card and there's state-of-the-art GPS for when I'm off-roading, there was no decision, to be honest."

The boys are stunned. But Sasha hasn't finished. She looks at Tommo. Sweeps her eyes over the rest of them. Back to Tommo. "In fact," she says, without a hint of a smile, "I'd say it gives pretty much the most pleasure you can get in public. Legally."

And she walks over to the girls, who high-five her.

"Sit here, Sash. And hey, I *love* your jeans."

"God, I hate you already, Sash – you're so slim I could get my hands around your waist and there'd still be room for something small."

They look over at the boys.

And laugh.

## What's going on in the brains of these teenagers?

In some ways, this isn't only about teenagers. This is about something which we are nowadays allowed to admit – that there are differences between male and female brains. They are differences that can be measured, tested in laboratories and seen on the fMRI scans of average males and females of all ages.

For many years scientists have argued about whether men and women seem different because they were born different or because they have different life experiences and are treated differently from birth. This is the "nature versus nurture" debate.

Until recently most scientists would have sat right on the fence and said that it's a bit of both and impossible to tell which has more effect. (Though for quite a long time during the twentieth century, most experts believed it was mostly nurture, or society and experience, and that the brains of baby boys and girls were the same.) But the more scientists look at real brains, the more they are inclined to say that there are some distinct differences, many of which can't be explained simply by what happens to us during our lives. Or whether we were dressed in pink or blue, or given dolls or trucks to play with. It is an inescapable fact that male and female brains

116

are different, biologically and physically.

We'll look at the differences in a minute, but first a warning: statements about male and female brains are about averages. They do not mean that every male brain behaves in a particular way and every female brain behaves in a different way. There is a great deal of overlap and one important thing to remember is this: if you are a girl and discover that your brain seems to work in a male way, this does not mean that you are less feminine; similarly, a boy whose brain works in a female way is no less masculine than any other. And it's not about being homosexual or heterosexual either.

So, what are the differences which the teenagers at the start of this chapter were showing? To what extent were the boys being boys and the girls being girls?

**OBSESSION WITH DETAIL AND SYSTEMS** – Professor Simon Baron-Cohen, in his fascinating book *The Essential Difference*, talks about the "systemizing brain" of the average male. You'll notice that the boys were very interested in and knowledgeable about the technical specifications of the phone, whereas the girls were more interested in the appearance and usefulness in a practical but not technical way. The new girl, Sasha, showed that girls can have a male-brain way of thinking too.

**SOCIAL SKILLS AND BONDING** – Simon Baron-Cohen talks about the "empathizing brain" of the average female. Girls and women tend to touch each other more, groom each other and use compliments to create and cement friendships; boys and men tend to play-fight, touching each other only in the context of aggression (whether pretend or not), and are less inclined to use emotionally supportive language with each other. Girls go shopping arm in arm – I've never seen boys do that.

Boys are also more prone to autism (though none of the boys in the scene showed signs of this). In fact, Simon Baron-Cohen describes autism as being an extreme form of male-brain behaviour. Autistic people lack understanding of social skills and bonding mechanisms.

**MENTAL MAP-MAKING** – When describing or remembering how to get to a particular place, female brains tend to remember landmarks and descriptions, while a male brain is more likely to construct a mental map and give directions involving distances and left/right instructions. Males are also better at estimating time and distance and visualizing shapes from different angles.

**VERBAL SKILLS** – Boys and men often have more difficulty expressing and explaining themselves in words. Girls and women tend to use a wider vocabulary, be more articulate and use more complex grammar. Boys and men are more prone to stuttering, being tongue-tied and every sort of language problem, including dyslexia. As you will see on page 120, females even use different areas of the brain from men when using language – they use both halves of the brain together, whereas men tend to use the left much more.

*These are the main differences which
researchers have identified as characteristics of the
average male and female brains:*

## Males
### AS BABIES/CHILDREN

- look at objects more than faces
- are attracted to toy vehicles as playthings
- utter their first word slightly later
- gurgle/babble less as babies, which may be practice talk
- make less eye contact
- have poorer concentration – will look at something for a shorter time
- have poorer fine motor skills – i.e. detailed manual work such as controlling a pencil

## Females
### AS BABIES/CHILDREN

- look at faces more than objects
- are more sensitive to noise, touch, taste and smell
- develop all language skills earlier, including first word
- gurgle/babble more as babies
- develop social skills better – feel a greater need to make friends
- have better concentration – stare at things for longer
- have better fine motor skills

# Males

- are more prone to stuttering and hesitate more during speech
- are more likely to have language problems, including dyslexia
- are more likely to have autism or Asperger's syndrome
- focus on how objects or systems work
- make obsessive lists – are more likely to be trainspotters, plane-spotters and birdwatchers, and to learn sports statistics
- are more likely to be psychopaths or murderers: murder of men by men is 30–40 times more common than that of women by women
- are better at judging space – and at throwing and aiming
- tend not to touch each other in affection/support
- are better at detecting small movements
- are less likely to try to get treatment for depression but more likely to commit suicide successfully
- are more likely to be exceptionally gifted – but are also more likely to have brain disorders

# Females

## AS ADOLESCENTS/ADULTS

- talk more, e.g. on the phone
- use more words, make fewer language errors, use longer sentences and more complex grammar
- talk about emotions more
- are better at noticing small differences in pattern, picture or colour
- are less interested in detail and statistics
- are likely to have a better diet and healthier lifestyle
- navigate using landmarks rather than mental maps
- like shopping together, being sociable
- are less prone to taking risks
- are more prone to depression and failed suicide attempts
- are more likely to retain a stronger memory in old age than males
- live longer

# The "alien face" experiment

Simon Baron-Cohen, in *The Essential Difference*, describes an amazing experiment devised by two of his research students, using 100 one-day-old babies.[29] At the time, the researchers did not know which of the babies were girls and which boys, so they couldn't be biased. They took a photograph of the face of one of the researchers. They then cut the photo up, rearranged the features and made it into a mobile which was unrecognizable as a face, though it contained exactly the same features. They called this the Alien. They showed the actual face and the Alien to the babies, and measured their responses. The girls looked for longer at the real face. The boys preferred the Alien.

Remember, these babies were one day old. They had had no time to be affected by the way people around them treated them as either boys or girls.

It seems from this experiment that it may be that females are naturally "people people", and males are naturally not. Parents and teachers may then need to approach boys and girls differently so that both sexes are given the opportunity to be as successful as possible in as many ways as possible.

## What do we see when we look at the male/female brain?

The male brain is on average 10% bigger – even after allowing for the difference in the weight of men and women. Traditionally, a bigger brain was supposed to mean a better brain, based on the fact that human brains are relatively bigger and heavier and cleverer than those of other mammals. However, before you boys get too excited, you need to consider a few things:

● Einstein's brain was no bigger than average – it actually weighed less and had a thinner cortex and fewer neurons compared to the supporting glial cells (though the neurons were more tightly packed together). His brain was apparently unusual in other ways: some parts seemed smaller, at least one part was missing, and at least one part appeared bigger, actually giving him a wider brain at one point. It's possible that we can't read too much into this – only certain parts were examined, and he was older than the brains with which he was being compared. However, we certainly can't say that having a bigger or heavier brain, or more neurons, is a mark of cleverness.

● Female brains have a greater proportion of grey matter – that's the information-processing bit.

- Also, remember the Australian anteater? The huge size of its frontal cortex hasn't got it very far.

So, size is not what counts – it's what you do with it. And most experts agree that women have the advantage in very many ways when it comes to brains. They are better protected against damage and less prone to problems such as autism, dyslexia, language difficulty, colour blindness, schizophrenia, attention deficit hyperactivity disorder (ADHD), Tourette's syndrome and virtually every brain disorder, both those which are there at birth and those which develop later in life. In later life, men lose brain cells faster and are more likely to develop memory problems.

Two other differences that scientists see when they look at the brain are that the two halves of the female brain tend to be more symmetrical and also that females tend to use both sides of the brain while using language. Males, on the other hand, seem to have a slightly larger right half of the brain and use the left side more than the right when using speech. Using both halves of the brain may explain why women tend to recover speech better after brain injury and find language easier in general.

fMRI scans show men usually only use the left side of their brains when doing a spelling or rhyming task, while women tend to use both sides at the same time.

Four other differences which researchers have detected between teenage girls' and boys' brains are:[30]

- the **amygdala** grows faster in teenage boys
- the **hippocampus** grows faster in teenage girls
- the **cerebellum** is 14% larger in boys than in girls
- the **basal ganglia** are larger in girls

## THE MALE VERSUS FEMALE TEENAGE BRAIN

*basal ganglia consist of several structures within here*

*amygdala grows faster in boys*

*hippocampus grows faster in girls*

*cerebellum is 14% larger in boys' brains*

So? Well, perhaps so nothing. But you could also note that the amygdala is largely responsible for "gut reaction" and primary emotion; the hippocampus is crucial in many memory tasks; the cerebellum is extremely important for physical coordination; and the basal ganglia help the frontal cortex work properly (and are also much smaller in people with Tourette's syndrome and ADHD).

## Sex Hormones

Hormones are a type of chemical in our bodies. Many are produced in the brain. They affect many aspects of our lives – from how we feel to whether we are male or female. They play a huge and essential part in sex differences, starting from time spent in the womb.

When a sperm fertilizes an egg, the embryo always starts out as a female. During the sixth or seventh week, hormones kick in, either turning the embryo into a male or keeping it as a female.
Boys – once upon a time you were female!

The main sex hormones are **testosterone** (mostly in males) and **oestrogen** (mostly in females). Normal males will have a small amount of female hormones, and vice versa.

127

Hormone levels change during our lifetimes, with huge activity during puberty when the differences between males and females become more obvious. They also change according to the season and, for women, during the menstrual cycle.

**OESTROGEN** – One effect of oestrogen is that it boosts dopamine. Dopamine can make the world seem rosier, brighter – but it can also make it seem darker, sadder. It can cause mood swings. However, it's important to realize that not all females have mood swings and not all mood swings are to do with sex hormones. Boys have mood swings too.

**TESTOSTERONE** – Increased testosterone causes aggressive behaviour. Studies have shown that testosterone increases during or after intense sport – especially if you are on the winning side (or if you are simply supporting the winning side as a spectator). Picture a gorilla beating its chest in an aggressive display of "look how strong and great I am" – this is what is happening in a male overloaded with testosterone.

If a girl has a condition called congenital hyperplasia, she has too much of the male hormone, testosterone. Such girls show more aggressive behaviour and better **spatial skills**, both of which are more common in males.

\* \* \* \* \*

## Environment

At the beginning of the chapter I mentioned the nature versus nurture argument, and then ignored it. I shouldn't ignore it: there's no doubt that boys and girls are often treated differently from day one. So it's hardly surprising if their behaviour ends up being different. And we've already seen that what you do makes a physical difference to your brain. It leaves a mark.

Maybe that's why there's a physical difference between the brain of a male and the brain of a female. Maybe it's all really caused by how you are treated – and if a girl is treated like a boy, she'll end up behaving like a boy and having a more "male" brain.

No. Take the fascinating, though tragic, example known as the John/Joan case. In 1967, twin boys were born. At a few months old they had to be circumcised for a medical reason, but something went terribly wrong and one of the babies had his penis accidentally destroyed. The devastated parents followed the advice they were given by an expert: that he should have a full sex change and be raised as a girl without ever being told the truth. John became Joan. Over the next 20 years, "Joan" had many operations and psychologists hailed this as a success story, saying that the child had happily been raised as a girl and suffered no ill effects. Many other children born with problems with their sexual organs ended up having sex changes purely because this case was supposed to have been such a success.

However, when "Joan" was 25, this so-called success story was revealed to be a terrible failure: "Joan" had been desperately unhappy as a girl and had endured a lifetime of teasing, confusion and sadness. When he discovered the truth, he chose to revert back to his true sex, that of a male. Nurture, or experience and upbringing, had completely failed to overcome biology.

Another "proof" appears when we look at other animals. The same sort of physical differences can be seen in the brains of male and female rats, for example: we see slightly larger brains in males, and more grey matter in females. But rats treat their newborn babies the same whether they are male or female – no pink or blue nurseries for them.

Certainly, what we do, what we experience, what we think and what we learn all affect our brains in physical ways, but they are quite small ways. Nothing compares to the strength of biology and genes. We can only work with what we've got – but we can work to improve it and use it as best we can.

# Why are Male and Female Brains Biologically Different?

### THE THEORY – IT'S EVOLUTION

The only way to answer this question sensibly is from an evolutionary angle. Someone might argue that the way we treat our babies moulds their brains to become more physically male or female, but it was evolution which determined our male/female roles in the first place so we have to start from there. We have to look back to early humans again – the different roles grew from the unavoidable fact that women have babies and men do not. In the hunter-gatherer societies of early humans, it worked better if males hunted wild animals and females gathered berries, fruit and other plants closer to home, and nurtured the babies which they bore and fed.

Males needed strength, the ability to travel long distances and find their way back, the ability to throw weapons accurately and judge the speed of a moving animal. Women needed to tell the difference between similar plants and remember which were poisonous or not; they raised the children and taught them skills; they had to work together in close social groups, bond and nurture; they needed to get on with each other. Also, men needed to compete for women, not the other way round – because a man would be more efficient at passing on his genes if he mated with several women, whereas a woman could only produce a small number of children and therefore needed to be very fussy about whom she mated with. Women used up a lot of energy having children (some things don't change) and men didn't, so women had more to lose and needed to choose a mate more carefully.

All these reasons can be linked with many of the differences which we see between male and female skills today. Over the huge amount of time that evolution takes, our brains have evolved differently because of the different roles and needs of males and females.

When my husband and I go to the supermarket, we act in ways remarkably similar to those hunter-gatherers: he goes charging off to the other end of the store and comes triumphantly back with one item, before rushing off to find something else. I go up and down the aisles carefully gathering all the items we need. If you left us both to our own devices, he would have a trolley full of random and probably very tasty (if expensive) things, and I would have a trolley containing all the boring things that we actually need. We are better dressed than the hunter-gatherers and my husband doesn't use a spear to capture the chocolate biscuits, but in other ways little has changed in more than 10,000 years.

# Fertility

If, like me, you are interested in asking questions and looking deeply into things, here's another fascinating difference. Adolescent girls start to look like fully grown women well before they are fully fertile. Adolescent boys do the opposite – they are fully fertile long before they look like fully grown men.

Let me explain. Women are not fully fertile until they are 19 – remarkably, 19 is the normal age for a first pregnancy in all cultures throughout the world and across all recorded generations. Yet adolescent girls develop their adult female shape long before this. Meanwhile, men are fully fertile while still adolescents, but they do not bulk up in terms of their muscles and skeletons until later – they still look relatively boy-like rather than manly until 18 at least.

Why? Why have nature and evolution given us these odd differences? With nature and evolution, we always need to look back to the earliest humans, because adaptation is a very slow process.

In early human cultures, adult males and females would have felt threatened by fully fertile adolescents of the same sex, because they would have been competing for mates. If they had felt threatened, they would not have spent time teaching and supporting them, and would have been more likely to fight and kill them (in the case of males) or exclude or suppress them (in the case of females). This is what actually happens among many other mammal groups – but it doesn't matter so much with other animals because their adolescence is short and they don't need to learn so much.[31]

So, the suggestion is that in early humans, adult females were not threatened by girls looking like women, because they were not fully fertile and therefore not a threat in terms of reproduction. So adult females were happy to teach social skills and how to bring up children. At the same time, adult males were not threatened by adolescent boys, because they looked weedy, so they were happy to teach them hunting skills.

Anyway, a long adolescence for humans, and the very different skills required in early males and females, could explain the biological differences in our brains.

### How are these differences relevant to teenagers today?

**LEARNING** – Different sexes may need different methods of teaching. For example, when teaching languages, some pupils (perhaps more often the boys) may need the rules and grammar explained in a very structured, systematic way. In science subjects, some pupils (perhaps more often the girls) may not grasp the underlying systems quickly or easily and may need more rote learning, practical examples or a more imaginative type of language, perhaps using comparisons and analogies.

How you learn for tests or exams may be different too. You may learn better when material is presented in the form of a picture or map; you may prefer lists with rhymes to help you remember.

**EMOTIONAL BEHAVIOUR** – Remember that test with the face showing fear (page 31)? Remember that the adolescents who got it wrong seemed to be using that emotional amygdala more than the prefrontal cortex? Well, some research shows that girls start to use their prefrontal cortex to control emotional activity earlier than boys. Boys may take longer to develop self-control.

**RISK BEHAVIOUR** – Boys do seem to take more risks, and more dangerous ones.

*Here are some of the things that adolescent boys seem to do more than girls:*

- not wear seat belts or motorbike helmets
- drive while drunk
- binge-drink and drink heavily. Some studies show that 69% of heavy drinkers are boys.
- use and deal drugs
- smoke
- fight and carry weapons
- have sex before 13
- overeat and consequently be overweight

\* \* \* \* \*

135

*Here are some of the things that adolescent girls seem to do more than boys:*

- have sex when they hadn't intended to
- fast or vomit to lose weight, take laxative or diet pills
- avoid physical exercise

Knowing about the different risks that boys and girls take should affect the type of social education that parents and teachers offer. Boys and girls are not the same and need different advice and strategies.

If you live with a single parent or carer of the opposite sex from you, he or she may not understand if you don't have the same skills, needs or learning methods. Now you can explain that males and females often have different ways of working and learning.

**BODY CHANGES** – Rather obviously, boys' and girls' bodies change in different ways. But the thing about girls looking like women before boys start to look like men is important: it sometimes means that girls begin to think they are fat, because their bodies are changing so quickly in outward ways. Understanding this is important – girls need to remember that these changes are about becoming a woman and are attractive.

When women are asked what sort of female body shape they think men most like, they usually get it wrong: in studies, researchers have shown pictures of women to men and women, asking the women which ones they think the men will fancy and asking the men which ones they actually do fancy. Women nearly always point to pictures of thinner women than the men choose. Women think men like them to be thinner than they actually do.

Of course, women and girls are not supposed to change their body shape to suit men, but actually this is what biology tells us to do. In the rest of the animal world, being attractive to the opposite sex is all that matters. It's the only way to pass on genes. Biology is strong in humans too, and most teenage girls do want to be attractive to boys (and the other way round) – but studies show that being skinny is not the way to do it.

Teenage girls (and girls even younger) often become too sensitive about weight. It is estimated that 60% of teenage girls are trying to lose weight at any one time. Very few (around 1–3%) develop the serious conditions of **anorexia nervosa** (self-starvation) or **bulimia** (binge-eating and vomiting). But many others risk damaging their long-term health by not eating enough of the nutrients they need, especially, in the case of girls, calcium and iron.

**BEING AN EARLY OR A LATE DEVELOPER** – The most difficult thing to deal with, for both boys and girls, is developing either much earlier or much later than others of the same age. For girls, developing early creates an extra risk of early sex and also alcohol addiction, as well as an increased risk of depression, eating disorders and anxiety (see Chapter Five).

For boys, early physical development can have benefits – you are likely to be more popular and be given leadership positions; the downside is that adults may expect you to be advanced in terms of school work too, which is unlikely because your frontal cortex is still not mature and may develop later than that of most girls.

**CLUMSINESS AND GROWTH** – For a long time, parents have noticed that teenagers can be extra clumsy. They can drop things, trip over things and become uncoordinated. Adults have always explained this by saying, "Oh well, it's hardly surprising – all that sudden growing means that their brains can't keep up with their arms and legs."

The real reason is maybe close, but a little more scientific – one of the areas of the brain which grow most in adolescence is the cerebellum, which is also very important in controlling large movements. It may be that the newly developing brain simply hasn't properly rewired itself following its sudden growth.

Teenage boys and girls usually have a growth spurt lasting around one year. Boys grow on average 4.1 inches and girls 3.5 inches during this time. Girls have this growth spurt on average two years before boys. During the growth spurt, weight will also increase, due mainly to muscle in boys and fat in girls. Again, these differences between boys and girls can cause problems with accepting the new body. This self-consciousness could make any clumsiness worse.

Stress can also cause clumsiness, and teenagers often have more stress than other groups. Adults, too, can find themselves being more clumsy or forgetful during times of stress – so it may not be entirely down to the teenage brain: it could be the whole life situation a teenager has to deal with, all those extra things to worry about, all overcrowding the brain. Hardly surprising if you accidentally spill the odd cup of coffee over your maths homework...

**MOVING TO SECONDARY SCHOOL** – On average, girls will probably be hitting puberty just as they start secondary school. This could make things extra difficult. On average, boys will hit puberty a little later, giving them time to settle in first.

**RELATIONSHIP TO OTHER-SEX PARENT** – At this time, a boy's relationship with his mother and a girl's with her father may change. You may not want to touch or be close to your other-sex parent and you may even find him or her repulsive. Don't worry about this (as if you were!) – there's a good biological and evolutionary explanation. In the animal kingdom, incest (sex between blood relatives) is a very bad idea as it can lead to deformities in offspring.

So, from a biological point of view, once you are becoming sexually mature, it is an advantage if you are NOT physically attracted to your parents. Rivalry and arguments between brothers and sisters also have the same benefit. Disliking your family is not a bad thing!

## "What can I do to help my male or female brain?"

Obviously there's not much you can do to make your brain more male or more female – and why would you want to? The differences are useful and fun and go towards making us all who we are. But I do have a few points:

● Knowledge is everything (almost), so just knowing *why* there are some things you find easier than others can help. You can then find strategies to help you in your areas of weakness. And you should not think you are "stupid" just because your friend finds a task easier than you.

● In intelligence tests, boys and girls or men and women do equally well – so forget about boys or girls being cleverer: we all have different strengths. Besides, intelligence tests only test certain types of intelligence. They don't test things like practical common sense or the important ability to relate to other people.

- Remember: this is about averages. Many female brains are brilliant at the things male brains are usually better at, and many male brains are fantastic at the things female brains are usually better at.

- Just because a friend of the opposite sex finds it easy to learn things one way doesn't mean you will – you may need different ways to remember or learn. Experiment with different methods, using "mind maps", colours, memory tricks, rhymes. Mind-mapping is a method of learning developed by Tony Buzan. It's very popular but may not work for you – you may do better by using rhymes to remember things.

- Whatever your weaknesses, they can and will improve with practice and good teaching – you can blame your brain for how you are but you can't blame it for how you will be! Remember: when you practise or try anything, your brain grows connections and gets better at it.

Your brain is especially "plastic" just now. In other words, it can be moulded or changed more easily. And the more different things you give it to do, the better. NOW is the time to make it brilliant.

# TEST YOURSELF

## Does your brain have male
## or female patterns?

This is more fun if you compare the results with some friends – boys and girls.

### ANSWER THESE QUESTIONS

**1** Which object is missing from one of these boxes?

**2** Which two shapes would be identical if turned the right way round?

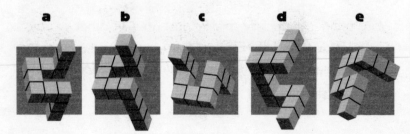

**3** *Find a watch or clock with a seconds hand so you can time 30 seconds exactly. You also need a piece of paper and a pen or pencil.*

**How many words beginning with *t* can you write down in 30 seconds? You do not need to spell them correctly.**

**4 Which two houses are identical?**

**5 Which of these three patterns contains the shape on the right?**

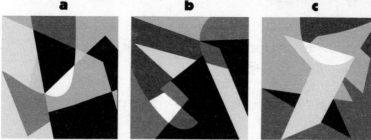

**6** Which two stars are identical if turned correctly?

a    b    c    d    e

If you did better at tests **1**, **3** and **4**, your brain has typical female skills. If you found tests **2**, **5** and **6** easier, your brain has typical male skills.

# CHAPTER FIVE

# The Dark Side – Depression, Addiction, Self-Harm and Worse

*"My life's not worth living."*

*Meet Gemma. She is fifteen. There is nothing funny about her situation. Her friends are worried about her. Her parents are worried too. Very worried. She's so beautiful and clever, they say, so why does she have to look so sad? She used to play in teams, be in the school orchestra, belong to clubs – now she's dropped everything. She doesn't care about her appearance, often doesn't wash her hair, doesn't use make-up or bother with nice clothes as she used to. They know she's been skipping school, and sometimes when they come home from work she's still in bed. They want her to see a doctor.*

Gemma is in her bedroom. The curtains are closed and a dim light bulb lifts the darkness to a dull mustard gloom. The heating is on but she feels cold. She is tired but she can't be bothered to get ready for bed. Maybe she'll just climb into bed with her clothes on.

She stares at her computer screen. She is supposed to be writing an essay. She has known that for days, and she knows all her friends have already done it. But she wasn't in school today. Well, she was at first, but she left at lunchtime, told someone to tell her teachers that she felt ill. She did feel ill. Sort of dead-headed. And not being in school seems like a good reason for not doing the essay.

Her English teacher says the essay is important. She needs it for this stupid thing called a portfolio, where you have to collect your best bits of work through the year and they go towards the exam. So? What's the point of that? Gemma's not going to be a writer. Or an English teacher. When will she ever need to "Compare and contrast the poems of Wilfred Owen and Siegfried Sassoon"?

Gemma still stares at the screen. She can't bring her fingers to move or her brain to think. There seems to be a gap between her head and the rest of her body. Distant noises in the house feel like another world, a world she doesn't belong to. And wrapped around her head is a heavy grey cloud, a shadow that sits hooding her eyes and making everything look dark and half visible.

Tears start to blur her vision. They come from nowhere.

Forget the essay. Gemma clicks the Internet connection and goes online. There's an Internet community she visits sometimes, a place where teenagers talk about anything and everything. A place to moan and gossip and sometimes even to laugh. They never meet each other, never see each other's faces, but she feels she knows them. She'll get chatting, and she'll feel better.

She logs on using her screen name, Pearlgem.

She scans the list of current topics. One catches her eye, traps the breath in her throat. "Anyone depressed out there? I need to talk," it says.

She clicks on it. There are three people logged into the chat room. Gemma begins to read the messages they've posted so far.

**Witchwoman07:** Hey, anyone out there being treated for depression? I need to talk. I just went to the doctor today after weeks of my stepmum nagging me, and hey, guess what, the doc says I'm depressed (like I didn't know) and have to take pills. And that has made me feel … yeah, you guessed, more depressed. It's official. Being told something like that's meant to make me feel better? So, what I wanna know is, anyone know how long these things take to work? And what if they don't?

**Sunflower000:** Hey, witchwoman, I'm sorry you're feeling bad. I had depression too, last year, and I had pills and I used to go see some person. Don't know if it was the pills or the talking, but after about 2 or 3 months I began to feel better. I really noticed it one day – like the cloud was lifted and the sun was shining again. Hey there, Mr Blue!

It wasn't the end of it – some days I'd feel bad again, but the sunny days did get more and more, like spring coming and it just gets a little warmer and a little lighter each day, you know? Hang in there – and if those pills don't help, some different ones will.

**Saintorsinner:** Hey, guys, can I join in? I don't know if I've got proper depression. Like, I don't sit and cry all day or go around saying, "I feel so depressed." But all this term I've felt sort of bored and empty, and half asleep, as though I really just can't be BOTHERED to do anything. I used to be a real party girl, and I was so into dancing (as in ballet, exams and stuff – yep, I was obsessed), but now I can't be bothered. And I can sit at my desk for an hour and I've done nothing, but then I don't even care that much – there's a bit of my brain that knows I should have done something, like homework, but the rest of my brain just says, "So?" Like today's Friday and my friends are going out, but I'm not because guess what? I can't be bothered. And it's not just in my head – it's my body too. It doesn't want to move. Couple of weeks ago my friend's father died and everyone was crying and everything for her, but I just couldn't think what to say and I didn't go into school for two days. I didn't cry or anything. I just felt kind of not there, like my brain had had an injection at the dentist's. I kind of know I should feel bad about not helping my friend, but I don't know, what could I do?

**Sunflower000:** I've heard of that sort of depression but mine was definitely the crying sort. I'd be having dinner with my family and all their voices would start crashing around my head and I'd feel this horrible sadness washing through me and I'd have to make an excuse

148

and leave the table. I'd just go up to my room and as soon as I shut the door the tears would just pour out. I'd sit on my bed with my arms around all my soft toys, all together like I'd never want to let them go, and I'd be sitting there with tears running down my face. They seemed to come from the deepest place where I couldn't even see, and sometimes this terrible quiet moaning noise would come out too – it was as if someone had died or everyone had died and I was the only person left in the world. But I didn't know WHY, cos if you'd asked, "Oh, so what's wrong with your life, then?" I couldn't even have answered. It wasn't in my head – it was in my heart, so deep, and all through my body, everywhere except my head. My head was a separate place. The sadness was in my veins, my skin, my lungs. Sometimes I could hardly breathe, it was weighing me down so much.

Gemma can't read any more. The tears are pouring down her face. She logs out without leaving a message. She sits on her bed, as she often does, just like Sunflower. Sunflower. Sunflowers are happy, bright, warm, they smile, they are tall and strong. But look at the sadness Sunflower was hiding. Gemma hugs her favourite soft rabbit tightly and buries her face in its clean baby smell, while all the tears just flow out. She lets them come.

After a while, Gemma stands up. She puts her rabbit down and goes downstairs. Taking a deep breath, she goes into the sitting room, where her mum is watching television.

"Mum," she says in a small voice.

Her mum looks up. She sees something is wrong and she quickly gets up and walks over to her daughter. Gemma does not move. Her shoulders droop.

"Mum, I need help," she says, and her face crumples again.

## What's going on in Gemma's brain?

Most teenagers go through adolescence without suffering like Gemma. Gemma certainly has depression, but she is on her way to recovery because she is going to get help. It is estimated that only 15% of depressed people get treatment – but of the people who do get treatment, at least 70% get better. Whatever the figures, there's definitely help out there if you need it.

How do you tell the difference between depression and "normal" sadness that anyone can feel every now and then? In real depression (clinical depression) the sad feelings go on and on for weeks. Anyone can have a day or two, or even three, feeling like Gemma, sometimes for a reason and sometimes for no obvious reason; but normally this passes and you feel fine again. In depression, it doesn't pass.

*Here are some of the symptoms:*
- feeling sad/angry all or most of the time; you may feel worse in the mornings
- feeling that you are worth nothing/ugly/useless, that you are a waste of space, that everyone would be happier if you weren't there
- not being hungry – or eating too much; losing weight or gaining weight (though some weight

gain during adolescence is essential – you are still growing)

- no longer enjoying things you used to enjoy
- sleep problems – difficulty getting to sleep, or waking very early and lying awake
- feeling tired all the time – really tired
- having problems concentrating; forgetting things a lot
- quite often thinking about what it would be like to die, thinking it might solve your problems, thinking about different ways of committing suicide

If one or more of those things describe the way you feel, get help. Even if you aren't sure, ask someone you trust: parent, carer, grandparent, friend, teacher, doctor. Anyone. Or if you want to speak to a stranger, there's ChildLine or the Samaritans. The phone numbers are at the end of this chapter.

Depression is extremely common among teenagers and adults. But it very often seems to start in the teenage years. Around 5% of children (7–12 year-olds) will have depression, but this rises to 15–20% of teenagers (13–18), which is similar to adults. It affects twice as many girls and women as boys and men.

Before looking at the teenage brain again, let's look at some of the other things that can sometimes (but not often) go badly wrong in adolescence.

**SUICIDE** – Of course, the worst result of depression is suicide, though most people with depression do not commit suicide. But in the UK suicide is the second most common cause of death in 15–24 year-olds, after accidents. It accounts for more deaths than cancer, leukaemia, heart disease, birth defects, strokes, lung disease and Aids added together. It is four times more common among boys and young men, though girls and women make more failed attempts.

If you ever think about taking your own life, talk to someone. Suicide is not the best way out and there is someone who can help you find a different way and enjoy the rest of your life. ChildLine and the Samaritans are there to help, among others. They do a fantastic job and are experts at helping people with suicidal thoughts.

153

**SELF-HARM** – Deliberately hurting yourself, by cutting or burning (the most common ways) or anything else, is usually called self-harming. It's one aspect of depression and it isn't just something that young people do. Some people who self-harm say they do it because in depression they feel nothing and hurting themselves makes them feel something. For others it's a way of telling people that they are unhappy. Others say it relieves anger or stress. Whatever the reason, it's obviously not a happy state to be in and, just as with all forms of depression, sufferers can get help. Don't be ashamed of self-harming – but do seek help. ChildLine and the Samaritans are good starting points.

**EATING DISORDERS** – Anorexia nervosa and bulimia are forms of self-harm. They are complicated conditions with lots of different causes and treatments. In very simple terms, anorexia nervosa involves not eating enough to stay healthy; bulimia involves eating large amounts and then making yourself sick to avoid the body absorbing the food. Both are very dangerous conditions and need medical help.

Sometimes eating disorders arise from thinking that you are fat. But often it is not as simple as that: sometimes it stems from trying to exercise control over the body when everything else in your life seems to be out of control. Most sufferers have very low self-esteem and this can be part of the cause. If you or someone you know suffers from either or both of these conditions, do please ask for help.

**SCHIZOPHRENIA** – This condition often begins in adolescence. It affects around 1% of the population at some time in their lives – though in many cases this will be just one episode which will not happen again. Boys and men have it more often than girls and women.

Schizophrenia is sometimes called "split personality", but this is not the correct way of thinking about it. People with schizophrenia sometimes can't tell the difference between reality and imagination and have very muddled thoughts which make them behave in a way that seems strange to other people. They may hear voices telling them to do something and find it very hard to ignore the voices.

*Here are some of the symptoms:*
- having strange beliefs – like thinking you have special powers
- seeing/hearing/smelling things that are not there – including hearing voices telling you to do something
- doing things that other people think are very weird and unacceptable – like taking your clothes off in public

- having thoughts that jump quickly from one thing to another in strange ways

Several studies have also shown that in schizophrenia the prefrontal cortex is not working normally. At the pruning stages of a normal teenage brain, around 15% of the grey matter (neurons) is pruned away from this area – in a schizophrenic patient there can be a loss of up to 25%. People with schizophrenia have symptoms a bit like people with damage to the prefrontal cortex – and as the teenage prefrontal cortex is going through so much change, it is easy to imagine that at this time your brain is particularly vulnerable to problems.

> **Long-term use of cannabis has been strongly linked to schizophrenia.**

**ADDICTION** – As I showed in Chapter Three, there's a higher risk of addiction during adolescence if you decide to start drinking, smoking or taking drugs. If you begin drinking heavily before the age of 15, you are four times more likely to become addicted than if you delay drinking till you are 21. It's the same for drug addiction. Drinking or taking drugs as a teenager is much more dangerous than doing it later.

If you are a girl and start puberty earlier than normal, this can make you more at risk of addiction, as well as more likely to have sex young. But lots of girls start puberty early and don't fall into that trap, so I don't think you can really blame your brain for that. It's more likely to be a showing-off response, as if you are saying to the world, "Look at my body – look what I can do!" Don't!

> A study using mice found that cocaine caused more damage to adolescent brains than to brains of adults or babies. Researchers believe that other drugs have a similar special effect on teenagers.[32]

## Why is the teenage brain more vulnerable to all these problems?

### THEORY 1 – CHANGES IN THE PREFRONTAL CORTEX

You know all about the growth and pruning of the prefrontal cortex by now! So, how might it affect some teenagers in these negative ways?

*Depression.* When you are depressed, you don't see things logically, you don't make good decisions, and you may be snappy and overemotional – all those things need a good prefrontal cortex to control them, and you don't have one yet. Is this why depression is common in adolescence? I don't think so. If it was the reason, we should see much more depression in teenagers than in adults – because an adult's prefrontal cortex is fully developed. But we don't – we see about the same amount of depression in both age groups. However, having an immature prefrontal cortex certainly can't help, and may make things worse. My point is that you may well have a confused prefrontal cortex at this stage, but it is not necessarily the cause of your depression.

*Suicide.* The rate of suicide in teenagers is higher than in adults, so maybe this extreme bad decision-making does have something to do with the prefrontal cortex. Suicide in a teenager is the ultimate bad decision – to end your life because at the moment life doesn't seem worth living. But round the corner is a much better answer – if you ask for help to find it. Don't allow that confused prefrontal cortex to let you down.

*Addiction.* Recent studies using fMRI techniques show that the teenage brain reacts differently from an adult brain to all drugs, including alcohol and tobacco. We don't know exactly why this is, but the complex activity in the prefrontal cortex and all the important restructuring that goes on in other parts of your brain could well play a part.

\* \* \* \* \*

## THEORY 2 – IT'S HORMONES

You know about all the hormones flooding around your body, especially during adolescence. Hormones certainly affect our moods. Perhaps some people who develop depression at this time are simply especially overwhelmed by these hormones. But depression is more than a temporary mood swing affected, for example, by the menstrual cycle. Depression lasts longer than that. Hormones may play a part, but they can't be the whole story.

Low testosterone in boys can lead to depression. So can low oestrogen in girls. However, researchers have discovered that this is not true in teenagers who have a good relationship with their families – so maybe your environment and things that are happening to you are more important than the chemicals in your teenage brain.

## THEORY 3 – IT'S DOPAMINE

Remember dopamine from Chapter Three? That's the neurotransmitter, or brain chemical, which makes us want to seek out pleasure and thrills, and which gives risk-takers their "high". And remember that dopamine levels are different in adolescence? They seem to be higher. But if dopamine is responsible for great pleasure, how come it's being accused of being responsible for depression?

The answer is that dopamine doesn't just make the world seem like a great place. It can also do the opposite. What can happen is that if the parts of the brain that react to dopamine get too much of it, they may become less sensitive to it, and then you can feel dull and uninterested in things which used to give you pleasure. It's like a bit of you becoming numb. What your brain really wants is the right balance of all its chemicals, and the teenage years are perhaps a time when balance is difficult to find.

*Addiction.* Researchers have found that the dopamine system in the brain is affected in adult addicts. And it's that same dopamine system which is going through such change in the teenage brain. It seems that adolescence is absolutely the worst time to be bombarding the brain with mind-altering drugs. Addictive drugs and alcohol cause massive surges of dopamine.

### THEORY 4 – IT'S CULTURAL

While scientists can argue about exactly what is happening in the brain of someone with depression, there's no doubt that the things going on around you can have a huge effect on your mood. It feels as though life is more stressful for teenagers nowadays – there are more decisions, more room for arguments and more is expected of you. Your parents, teachers and carers may be more stressed too, rushing around and working harder and harder to earn money – and their stress can make life more tense at home.

And there are many things which are not new, but which are stressful for young people all the same: divorce or family break-up, moving schools, your changing body, the death of a friend or family member, bullying, illness, exams. These are things which anyone can find stressful but perhaps for teenagers it is worse – adults can find ways to deal with a difficulty or see their way through it, and young children have parents or carers to look after them, whereas teenagers feel they are becoming independent – which can be a frightening thought.

So being a teenager is stressful, even without everything that's going on in your brain. And stress can often lead to depression.

*Addiction.* Can stress lead to addiction? It can certainly make people turn to alcohol or drugs, thinking that this is a way out. And that, obviously, can lead to addiction.

*Schizophrenia.* Schizophrenia does often seem to start after a very stressful period or incident (though it's a bit hard to be sure, because there are lots of stressful periods during this time and most people do not get schizophrenia). But the extra stress of adolescence could be one reason why it seems to start during this time.

### THEORY 5 – IT'S EVOLUTION: DEPRESSION IS GOOD FOR US

What? Depression good for us? Surely not! Well, remember that an evolutionary biologist looks back to the earliest humans. Let's look back at them too.

First (and this isn't just about teenagers), you've probably heard of SAD, seasonal affective disorder, or winter depression. Well, maybe it's a throwback to our early human days when winter was a period when food wasn't so available, too much activity used up too much energy so people needed more food, and darkness was dangerous, a time when going to sleep was the best option. So, going slow, sleeping and shutting down the body could be the natural human way of dealing with winter. Lots of animals sleep all winter, after all – maybe tortoises simply have an extreme form of winter depression!

Second (and this *is* just about teenagers), in Chapter Two you saw that sleep patterns alter in adolescence, with teenagers needing more sleep. In some types of depression, it is as though the body is shutting down, saving energy, wanting to sleep more. If an adolescent needs more sleep, being depressed would be one way for the human adolescent in early times (and now) to get it.

**Not sleeping enough can lead to depression – one study has shown that insomniacs are 40 times more likely to become depressed.**

Third, there's another possible connection with evolution. For humans and other animals, one of the important natural instincts is "fight or flight". This describes the sudden massive stress which surges when a human or other animal confronts a dangerous or frightening situation.

You know the symptoms; you'll have had them yourself whenever you've had a shock, or a lion has leapt out at you from behind a tree (if that's never happened to you, just imagine it anyway): your heart starts beating very fast, you sweat, and all your senses become alert. You also gain extra strength – have you ever been chased by something that you were frightened of? I was chased by a goose once (don't laugh – they are scary beasts) and I jumped over a five-foot gate. Afterwards, I looked back at the gate and said, "Wow! How did I ever do that?" The answer is that my fight or flight response was working extremely well and the chemicals which rushed instantly round my body gave me extra strength. Luckily for the goose, I chose flight.

What has this got to do with depression and evolution? Maybe some sorts of depression developed as a reaction to too much constant stress. Constant stress is bad for us, all that cortisol and **adrenalin** putting a strain on our hearts and draining us of energy. Depression, and shutting down the body, could be the body's way of protecting itself, a method of keeping the world out and saying, "OK, I've had enough. I'm going to sleep till it's all over."

Now, you are probably thinking, But if a lion is running towards me and my body decides to opt out and go to sleep, that's not exactly an example of depression being good for me. No, I agree. But remember a couple of things:

163

- Evolution takes a very, very, *very* long time to change things and society changes much faster.
- Early humans would have released their stress by either fighting or fleeing, whereas today we usually don't have to do either of those things – perhaps it's this constant niggling stress that builds up and builds up without our being able or needing to do what our bodies are designed to do: fight or flight. Evolution just hasn't caught up with modern life yet.

So, make sure you don't meet a lion when you're feeling depressed. On the other hand – it might be just what you need to get you going...

## "What can I do to help my troubled teenage brain?"

- If you think you are suffering from any of the problems in this chapter, do ask for help. There are answers for everything if you speak to the right person.

- Be nice to yourself – the best advice I was ever given when things were getting me down was to give myself small rewards every now and then. It could be anything from a bar of chocolate (not too often, but chocolate does contain phenylalanine, an ingredient which boosts your mood) or a relaxing bath, to a meal out with friends, a trip to the cinema, or buying that CD you've wanted ever since your parents refused to get it for you – you know, the one with the *Parental warning: explicit lyrics* sticker.

- Realize that depression makes you see things in a warped way, a wrong way – you think you are ugly/ stupid/unpopular/too fat/too skinny or that you will never be a success; but it's not reality, just the way your brain is working. The mirror does lie.

- Never use alcohol, drugs or tobacco as a way to make you feel better – they won't.

- Vitamins – the B vitamins are especially important for mood. Vitamin B3, or niacin, helps the body make **serotonin**, a brain chemical which produces a feeling of quiet happiness (unlike dopamine, which gives the thrill feeling). You can take them as supplements, but it's even better to get them from foods: fortified cereal (fortified means with added vitamins, which should be listed on the packet), Marmite/Vegemite, rice, nuts, milk, eggs, meats, fish, fruits, leafy green vegetables and, most delicious of all, liver. Vitamin B6 may also be useful for girls whose mood swings relate to the menstrual cycle; you find it in fortified cereal, beans, baked potatoes, bananas, fish and tomatoes.

- Exercise is also very good for depression and mood swings – though you won't feel like doing it. Ask a friend to make you exercise. Once you force yourself to do it, you'll feel better about yourself.

- Never forget: everything is a phase. You think you'll feel like this forever but I promise you won't. Things change; light appears; adolescence does come to an end.

> **A cup of cocoa sounds comforting – and maybe it really is. Hot milk contains tryptophan, which not only helps you sleep, it also helps the body produce the calming chemical, serotonin. Turkey is another great source of tryptophan – maybe that's why we sleep and feel content after the Christmas/Thanksgiving meal.**

This has been a gloomy chapter. But remember that most teenagers will not experience these extremes. It's always useful to turn the facts around: if 15–20% of teenagers suffer from depression, that means that 80–85% won't. Your amazing brain will most likely carry you through.

# Useful contacts

ChildLine: Tel. 0800 11 11; **www.childline.org.uk**

Samaritans: Tel. 08457 90 90 90; **www.samaritans.org.uk**

Mind: **www.mind.org.uk** (this includes up-to-date statistics)

# TEST YOURSELF

### Are you feeling blue?

If you think you might be suffering from depression, you must seek proper help.

This questionnaire is not supposed to take the place of a visit to the doctor. But if more than one or two of these things have been true for you for more than a week, you should get help. Start by speaking to an adult whom you feel comfortable talking to.

**I do things slowly. I can't be bothered to do anything.**

**It's difficult to concentrate on work or reading.**

**I often can't make decisions.**

**I feel sad/gloomy quite often, sometimes for no reason.**

**Even when nice things are happening, I still feel sad.**

**I feel very tired. I seem to have no energy.**

I don't find any pleasure in things I used to enjoy.

I am agitated, fidgety, keep moving around.
I feel I am a failure.

I am a horrible person. I need to be punished.

I am sleeping badly – either having trouble
getting to sleep or waking up often and being
unable to get back to sleep.

I want to sleep a lot.
I often fall asleep when I shouldn't.

I sometimes think about the method
I would use to kill myself.

I often think about dying.
Sometimes I think people
would be happier if I were dead.

I have lost or gained weight without trying to.

## Do you have an alcohol problem?

Again, this is not meant to be a proper or complete test for whether you have a problem. Just answer the questions honestly and see what happens.

**1  Have you ever felt bad or guilty about drinking alcohol?**

**2  Have you felt irritated when people have criticized you for drinking too much?**

**3  Do you sometimes think perhaps you should cut down?**

**4  Have you been drunk more than once in the last month?**

**5  Have you more than once in the last year done something while drunk that you regret doing?**

**6  Do you feel that getting drunk is not really going to do you any harm as long as you stick with friends who will look after you?**

If you answered yes to even one of these questions, and you are younger than 18, it is very possible that you are drinking too much or that you have an unhealthy attitude towards alcohol. Your behaviour with alcohol now affects your future, but it is never too late to get help.

# CHAPTER SIX

# Getting Brighter – Your Brilliant Brain

*"Yes, Miss de Beauvoir, but surely you don't believe that existentialism holds the only real answer in a postmodern world?"*

*Meet Michael and Laura. They are twins. They are nearly seventeen. They have a younger brother, Ian, who is thirteen. It's Sunday evening and the family are finishing their meal. Laura has announced that she wants to be a psychiatrist.*

"God, Laura, why d'you want to work with a load of loonies?" says Michael, reaching for some more bread to mop up the gravy.

"I thought you wanted to be an engineer?" says their father.

"Yes, I know. I did. But I just think that's not really the way my mind works. I am more interested in thinking about reasons and looking at the whole picture. Yes, I know I've always liked working things out, but now I realize that I prefer working things out about people, not just machines and objects. Anyway, the brain is the ultimate machine, isn't it?"

"What's to work out about loonies?" says Ian. "Just get the men in white coats to deal with them." And he grins at Laura, before taking another mouthful of spaghetti and sucking it up, leaving tomato sauce all over his lips.

"Don't be silly, Ian," scolds their mum.

Ian laughs. He slouches in his chair and wipes his mouth with his hand.

"Anyway, you'll be used to loonies after living with Ian," says Michael.

"Loony yourself, fart-face," retorts Ian, throwing some bread at his brother.

"Stop it, Ian," orders their father crossly.

"Don't call them loonies," says Laura. "It's not their fault if something goes wrong in their brain. If you became mentally ill you'd want people to treat you decently and try to cure you. You'd want a hotshot psychiatrist like me."

"Quite right, Laura," says their mum. "Ignore Ian. He's just a silly boy."

Ian makes a V-sign at his mother, but luckily she doesn't see.

"So, when did this idea start?" asks their dad.

"We've been doing this taster course in philosophy and it really got me thinking – I mean, how do we know what's real, and who's to say our idea of reality is the right one? Who says who's mad and who's sane?

And how do we know what's in someone else's head? Then this week we had a talk from a neuroscientist, who argued that our personalities are nothing more than the chemicals and the cell structures in our brain. It got me thinking that we *must* be more than that, and somewhere between philosophy and science is the answer. Like to our whole identity."

Michael is looking at her with interest but complete lack of understanding. Her parents are looking at her in amazement. Ian is yawning and muttering, "Blah blah blah rhubarb rhubarb rhubarb crap crap crap."

"Be quiet, Ian, for goodness' sake," snaps their father.

"Yeah, well," mutters Michael, "I think shrinks are interfering busybodies. Remember I had to see one when I got chucked out of school last year?"

"Yes, Michael, how could we forget?" comments his dad drily. "You didn't exactly give the poor woman a chance, did you? I mean, you sat there in silence the first time and the second time you swore at her."

"Whoa, dude! Way to go!" shouts Ian, grinning and hitting the table with his fist so that his plate rattles and his fork falls onto the floor, splashing tomato sauce all over Laura's jeans.

"God, you'll be my first patient at this rate. You're completely off your rocker. These were clean on today and now look at them."

174

"Oh, boohoo," grumbles Ian, knowing he's in the wrong but unable to say sorry – because that would be humiliating.

"Right, Ian, leave the table immediately. I've had enough of your behaviour. You don't think of anyone but yourself! And it's your turn to do the washing-up," snaps their mother.

"It's not my turn! It's Laura's, and you know it!"

"Well, it's your turn now."

"That's so unfair! Why's it my turn?"

"Because I say so. You've just messed up Laura's jeans through your stupid carelessness, so the least you can do is the washing-up. Teach you to be more careful."

"Cow!" mutters Ian.

"What did you say?" demands their father.

"Nothing."

"Yes, you did. What did you say?"

"I just said *cow*, OK? Big bloody deal!"

"Apologize to your mother! Right now!"

"No bloody way! She picks on me. She *is* a cow! I'm only telling the truth. What do you want me to do? Lie? Oh, all right then, I'm *so* sorry and you *are* the most wonderful mother in the whole world!"

Ian storms out of the room, slamming the door.

The others look at one another.

Michael speaks first. "You shouldn't let him talk to

175

you like that, Mum. It's bang out of order."

His mother gives him a funny look – a smile, but a smile heavy with meaning. Michael looks back at her. Why is she smiling at him like that?

Then realization dawns. "Oh, right! I used to speak to you like that, didn't I?"

"Yes, and not so long ago." She is grinning now, as though a light has been switched on – for her it's a glimmer of light at the end of a tunnel; for Michael it's a sudden ability to see himself, how he is changing, and how he used to be. He is looking at himself from the outside.

Their father speaks. "Laura? How long does it take to become a psychiatrist?"

"Only about ten years."

"Any chance you could do it a bit more quickly, so you can tell us poor parents the answers to what the hell is going on in a teenage brain?"

## What's going on in the brains of
## Ian, Michael and Laura?

Ian, Michael and Laura illustrate the three different stages of teenage brain development and behaviour.

Ian, at 13, is in early adolescence. He is volatile, clumsy, risk-taking (calling your mother a cow is very risky behaviour) and often self-centred. He sometimes makes bad decisions, can't understand the viewpoints of others, and doesn't think things through in a mature and logical way. If you looked in his brain, you'd probably see lots of extra cell growth, all those new bushy branches of dendrites and synapses not really knowing what to do with themselves. And you might see more use of that gut-reacting amygdala and less use of the prefrontal cortex.

Michael, at nearly 17, is the same age as Laura. But he's a boy, and most boys do all this maturing a year or two later. He is starting to show an interest in things outside himself – for example, he has suddenly realized that he used to give his parents a hard time (he probably still does sometimes, but he's gradually learning self-control and more often makes good decisions). If you looked in his brain, you'd probably see that most of the pruning has now happened – the branching dendrites are clearer, less bushy than in Ian's brain. He has developed skills that he didn't have a few years ago and parts of his brain are working well together. But the branches aren't very strong yet. That's the next stage for him.

Laura, a nearly 17-year-old girl, is definitely reaching the end of the tunnel. She can understand abstract thoughts – in other words she can think about things she can't see, touch or hear, such as belief, ideas, truth, reality. She can understand her own learning abilities; she can look ahead and plan. In her language ability she has leapt ahead of both her brothers and she feels equal to her parents in her ability to think and hold an argument. If you looked in Laura's brain you would see about 15% less grey matter than you would in Ian's brain – yet hers is working much better than his. You might also see evidence of something which I have so far only mentioned briefly: myelination, or strengthening, of the white matter in the brain.

## Myelination

Myelin is a fatty substance that coats the long axons, the tail-like parts of a neuron which allow it to communicate with other neurons far away. It's like the insulation on an electric wire. And what it does is strengthen the pathways so that messages get through more effectively. It can only occur if the axon is not first deleted – and axons will be deleted if they are not used regularly. So, plenty of connections used regularly mean that the axon does not die and can therefore be myelinated. Once this strengthening myelination has happened on the axon, those neurons are less likely to fall away or weaken – explaining why practice really can make perfect.

Obviously myelination is good because it is strengthening, but actually the immature brain of Ian has one advantage: because he still has lots of extra neurons, dendrites and synapses, he has more options of things that he may learn easily. Since Laura's extra branches have been pruned away and have now been strengthened by myelin, she can still learn new things, but it will be slightly harder for her. Her skills and weaknesses are more fixed than Ian's and, to a lesser extent, Michael's. She will be very good at the things she's becoming good at now, but she perhaps has fewer choices than her brothers.

## Leaps and bounds

Many teachers and parents notice sudden huge improvements in teenagers' abilities during the later teenage years. And many teenagers notice this themselves. Suddenly you may "get" something you hadn't been able to do before.

If you were able to look into your brain at these moments, you might see new areas where the branches were all pruned and covered in their fatty myelin overcoats. A new piece of knowledge, a new ability, a new understanding, each one laid down to be useful to you in the future.

## "Is all this automatic? Can I just sit back and wait for it to happen?"

Unfortunately, no. Unless you want your only skill to be "supreme excellence at operating a TV remote control" – and you are probably excellent at that already. The brain operates on a "use it or lose it" basis – it develops networks because you try something, do something, learn something, practise something. The more you do, and the more different activities you take part in, the better your brain will be at those activities, and the better it will work in general, because a good brain is one where all the parts work well together.

Researchers tested some rats: they gave one group of rats some toys; they also gave them some other rats to keep them company, so that they had lots to do and some interesting occupations in their day.[33] They gave another group of rats nothing: no toys and no other rat companions. A few months later, the researchers looked at the brains of each group. They found some physical differences: the busy rats had a thicker cortex (mostly the grey matter or neurons) and many more glial cells – the cells that provide food for the neurons and support them. The researchers also believed that there were more synapses and dendrites, though they could not count them.

The lesson is that busy means brainy – the more you do, the more you can do.

**If you looked inside the brain of a violin player, you'd find extra dendrites and synapses in the area which controls the left hand's fingers.**[34] **The person did not become a violin player because of this extra growth – the cells grow and connect because of all the finger-moving. You can alter your brain.**

Research shows that at certain stages in our lives there are major growth spurts in numbers of neurons: these seem to happen at 4, 8 and 11 weeks; 4, 8 and 12 months; and 2, 4, 7, 11, 15 and 19 years. Some of these do correspond to "windows" – times when it seems that we need to learn something or we will never learn it (such as learning a language by the age of 7 – see page 14). It's as though the cell growth occurs to give the brain the opportunity to learn particular skills.

So, as an adolescent, the ages of 11, 15 and 19 may be the ages when you need to cram your life with lots of activity and new experiences, so that your brain can grow as brilliantly as possible. The trouble is, these are only average ages – your brain growth spurts may happen at 12, 16 and 20. Or 13, 17 and 21. There's only one safe answer – keep that brain stimulated all the time!

Slobbing in front of the TV is not good for you – official!

# What other brainy abilities do older teenagers gain?

**UNDERSTANDING JOKES** – Of course younger children and teenagers get jokes too, but the types of jokes that you get or enjoy will change. They'll probably also change during your adult life too, as you meet new people and have new experiences. The types of TV programmes you find funny will change. There is a significant and scary chance that you may even find some of the same things funny as your parents. I'm not joking.

**MAKING CONNECTIONS** – You may find that you will hear something or learn something, and suddenly be able to link it with something completely different. You may be discussing something in religious education and suddenly make a connection with something in history, or politics, or philosophy, or music.

**TWO DIFFERENT THINGS CAN BE TRUE AT THE SAME TIME** – You start to see that ideas and truths are not necessarily black and white. You realize that a sensible person can hold two beliefs that seem to contradict each other. For example, you may suddenly understand that yes, your parents do trust you and your boy/girlfriend, but that nevertheless they will not let you sleep in the same bedroom. You can see the wider picture – even if you don't like it.

**THEMES AND DEEPER MEANINGS** – Your ability to appreciate books, plays, poetry, art and subtle language will develop, sometimes suddenly. It's noticeable that in schools where there is streaming by ability between the ages of 15 and 17, the top English groups will usually contain more girls than boys – the boys have often not reached this level of language maturity yet.

**BIG IDEAS OF YOUR OWN** – Older teenagers are better able to build their own beliefs. Up till this point, you will usually believe what the people around you are saying – your parents, or a teacher, or a role model – or something you hear on television. Or you may hold a very strong opinion which is more a gut reaction than something you have worked out. But gradually your own views start to develop and you find you have your own system of beliefs. Your beliefs can still change, and probably will change during your life, but they now change when *you* decide.

It's no coincidence that in democratic countries the age of voting, the age of legal drinking and smoking, and the age of sexual consent range from 16 to 21, depending on the issue and the country. It is between these ages that you become really able to decide for yourself what is best for you.

## "Why do our brains work so much better at the end of adolescence?"

Let's see again the different ways of looking at reasons. Remember how they are all linked, and that evolution is the fundamental cause of our biology and therefore much of our behaviour.

### THEORY 1 – BECAUSE WE ARE WELL TAUGHT

Perhaps all this clever development and these new powers happen because we are well taught. Perhaps it's because we have a horrible number of years at school that we become so clever.

Well, brains certainly do change when they learn and practise new things, but this isn't enough to explain such dramatic brain changes – or why the same changes probably happen in all human societies around the world, whether or not people spend their childhoods at school. Without the proper brain development, no amount of wonderful teaching is going to turn you into a brilliant thinker, or writer, or mathematician, or basketball player.

It's interesting that you sometimes hear of children who are extraordinarily brilliant at maths passing their senior school exams and going to university aged 10 – but you never hear of the same thing happening with language. The human brain just doesn't do that, no matter how brilliant the early teaching might be. So, I would argue that we become clever mainly because our brains mature in such a way, not that our brains grow in such a way mainly because we learn things at school (though you can certainly improve the way your brain works, and even change it in some ways).

### THEORY 2 – IT'S EVOLUTION

This theory puts it the other way round: that our clever brains gave humans an advantage, so clever brains were passed on down the generations. Our complicated human society was able to become more and more complicated and successful because of our brilliant brains, and so brains became even more brilliant.

Humans can be musicians, plumbers, designers, politicians, doctors, cleaners, athletes, engineers, academics, writers, singers, cooks, philosophers, gardeners – the list is endless. We can be risk-takers if we want to be. We can have hobbies. We can relax on holiday or go white-water rafting. With every generation, human knowledge grows and is passed on, through parents, teachers, books – though some of it dies as well. Our societies are incredibly complicated, with some of us living in cities and others in villages or the country, some of us in democracies and some of us in dictatorships, some of us at war and some of us at peace. We have been to the moon.

You can't say the same about any other animals. Other

animals do what they are programmed to do on a day-to-day basis, in order to survive long enough to pass on their genes to the next generation. We do so much more.

To do all this, we need an absolutely fantastic brain. A brain so clever that it can look inside itself – something else that other animals don't do. So, we have a long childhood and a long adolescence and, during that adolescence, our brains grow so much that we could be everything, from pianist to politician, from cook to computer scientist. But as individuals we don't need to be everything – and there wouldn't be time in the day. So our brains prune away what we don't need, then strengthen what we use a lot, giving us, by the time we are adults, brains that can do some things brilliantly. Brains that allow us to function in our endlessly complicated society, so that we can pass on our genes down the generations – if we want to. And, in fact, perhaps the ultimate proof of our brilliant brains is that we have beaten evolution: we can now choose not to do what all animals are programmed to do – reproduce.

# TEST YOURSELF

## Test your brain power

Here are some questions which need your brain to work in different ways. Take your time, and use a pencil and paper if you want. Don't panic – it's meant to be fun!

**1**  **Which is the odd one out?**

*believe*    *say*    *hope*    *think*    *feel*    *decide*

**2**  **What would the next number be?**

*1*    *2*    *3*    *5*    *8*    *13*    *21*

**3**  **What would the next letter be?**

*A*    *D*    *C*    *F*    *E*    *H*    *G*    *J*    *I*

**4** Put two letters in each space, so that a new word is formed from the word on the left and a new word from the word on the right:

(*Example: LAD _L E_  APT = LADLE and LEAPT*)

**FINE** _ _ **RIPE**          **BUN** _ _ **IN**

**5** Pen is to ink as car is to

*garage    drive    key    petrol    fuel tank*

**6** If I weigh 75% of my own weight + 13 kg, how much do I weigh?

**7** Karim is shorter than Mark. Mark is taller than Sam. Which of following is certainly true?

(a) *Karim is taller than Sam.*
(b) *Sam and Karim are the same height.*
(c) *Karim is shorter than Sam.*
(d) *It is impossible to tell which of Karim and Sam is taller.*

**8** Read these statements:

(a) *Some politicians are liars.*

(b) *All liars have small ears.*

*If both statements are true, does this mean that some small-eared people must be politicians?*

Now turn over the page
for the answers and analysis.

**1** *say*: it is the only one spoken aloud, rather than silently thought.

**2** *34*: each number involves adding the two previous numbers. This is a Fibonacci sequence, and appears in lots of aspects of maths and nature.

**3** *L*: the sequence is: three forward, one back, three forward, one back, etc.

**4** *ST (FINEST and STRIPE)* and *CH (BUNCH and CHIN)*.

**5** *petrol*: a pen uses ink in order to work and a car uses petrol in the same way. And ink is the fluid in a pen and petrol is the fluid in a car.

**6** *52 kg*: 13 kg must be 25% of the whole weight – because we are told that 100% of the weight is made up of 75% + 13 kg. If 13 kg is 25% of the weight, the whole weight must be exactly four times that, because 100% is 4 x 25%. And 4 x 13 = 52.

**7** *d*: it is impossible to tell because all we know is that Mark is taller than both Sam and Karim, but we don't know which of them is taller.

**8** *Yes*: everyone who lies has small ears and some of those liars are politicians, so they must have small ears. There may also be some politicians who don't lie and some people with small ears who are not politicians.

Which were the ones you had most difficulty with? Did some of them feel easy and some of them make your brain squirm with confusion? Did some of them make you panic before you'd even tried to work them out? Did you choose to use pen and paper to help you? Did you use trial and error or did you use some logic to work them out? Did you prefer the number ones or the letter/word ones? Which did you like doing?

There are many different skills which come together to make your intelligence. Verbal (word-based) skills, number skills, logical reasoning, seeing patterns and sequences, spatial skills (see pages 142–4), memory, general knowledge, being able to categorize and compare and note differences – these are all things we need in order to be as intelligent as possible. They are all skills which we can improve with practice, guidance and help. We all have things we feel we are better at, and things we feel we are less good at – but all our weaknesses can be strengthened if we want them to be.

On the other hand, some of our greatest inventors or geniuses have not scored highly on IQ tests. Sometimes they are so brilliant in one area that they neglect the other areas. Maybe that's not so bad. Maybe we need some people to be extra brilliant at one or two skills. Maybe you will be one of those people. Good excuse for giving up on ... no, I mustn't say it.

Whichever questions you found easiest, think about the skills they seemed to need and see if you can find puzzle books or websites that will give you even more practice for those well-wired parts of your brain that make these things easy for you. But it will be an even greater help to you if you recognize the areas which were harder for you and practise those ones even more. Because, if there's one thing that this book should have told you, it's that you can change your brain by doing, by practising and by trying. Psychologists would also say by believing – and I believe they are right.

That wise ancient Greek philosopher Plato and his followers had a motto: Know Yourself. It's a great motto, but here's a better one: Grow Yourself.

For further information and lots of intelligence (IQ) and personality tests, try these websites:

**www.mensa.org.uk**
**www.queendom.com**
**www.intelligencetest.com**
**www.iqtest.com**

But for a really mind-opening way to get your brain working and help you be a brilliant thinker, try this book: *The Philosophy Gym* by Stephen Law – subtitled *25 Short Adventures in Thinking.*

# Conclusion

The human brain is an amazing thing, a mass of grey stuff which allows you to do every single thing you do, to think every thought you've ever had, which keeps you alive, and which makes you who you are, someone unique – different from every other person in the whole world. Yet there are things your brain does which are the same for all humans – and one of the essential things your brain does is to insist that you are, for a few years, a teenager, an adolescent.

The more I think about adolescence and the more teenagers I meet, the more I'm struck by what a very special time it is and how much you have going on in your lives and in your brain. I am full of respect for what many teenagers have to deal with and how you cope. One of my reasons for writing this book was that I want other adults to understand, to stop for a while and think.

Your brain is who you are and it is also who you will be. You own your brain and most of the time it is more or less in your control. And understanding more about your brain, as you do now, helps you have control. Only sometimes, when you can't do anything about it, when your brain takes over and biology rules, can you fairly shout, *"Don't blame me – blame my brain!"*

As a teenager, you will no doubt shout it as loud as you can.

# Glossary

**adolescence** time of change between child and adult; approximately from ages 10 to 18

**adrenalin** hormone especially linked to fear and excitement; increases heart rate

**amygdala** tiny part of limbic system within brain; linked to gut reaction and instinct

**anorexia nervosa** eating disorder where sufferer dangerously restricts food intake to lose weight

**axon** long, tail-like part of a neuron. Axons send messages to other neurons

**basal ganglia** consist of several structures deep inside the brain. Very complex, seem to affect movement, including skills like playing the piano, as well as other areas of brain activity

**bulimia** eating disorder where sufferer binge-eats and then vomits so as not to increase weight. Linked to anorexia. Literally means "ox hunger"

**cerebellum** part of the brain important for coordination and movement, some types of memory and aspects of speech. Literally means "little brain", because it looks like a small brain inside the brain

**cortex** outer layer of the brain, mostly neurons/grey matter. Only about 2 millimetres thick

**cortisol** a hormone known as the stress hormone

**dendrite** a branch from a neuron. Dendrites receive messages from other neurons by connecting through synapses

**dopamine** a neurotransmitter involved in our desire to seek thrill/ pleasure, e.g. with food, sex, risk-taking, new experience

**frontal cortex** the front areas of the cortex, containing the prefrontal cortex as well as motor cortex and other areas

**glial cells** much of your brain is made of glial cells, simple structures which scientists believe have the job of holding everything together and eliminating dead cells

**grey matter** mostly neurons, mostly found in the cortex. Regarded as the most important cells in your brain

**hippocampus** part of the brain very important for many aspects of memory. Literally means "sea horse", because of its shape

**hormone** hormones are special chemicals which affect us in many ways. Some are produced in the brain, others are not – but all are regulated from the brain. Each has a special job and affects things like behaviour, mood, stress and male/female behaviour

**limbic system** areas of the brain responsible mostly for emotional and unconscious or reflex behaviour. Sometimes called the "reptilian" brain, as reptiles and other non-mammals have one, whereas only mammals have a cortex

**melatonin** a brain chemical which controls your body clock and how sleepy you are

**mirror neuron** a type of neuron which acts when we simply watch someone else perform an action. It mirrors the action, enabling us to practise simply by watching

**neuron** the most important type of brain cell – you have about 100 billion

**neurotransmitter** a chemical produced at a synapse, allowing messages to be passed between neurons. About 50 different neurotransmitters have been discovered, each having a special job within its own system of cells. Dopamine is an example

**oestrogen** a sex hormone found mostly in females, important for female body characteristics and behaviour

**prefrontal cortex** the front-most area of the frontal cortex, essential for the ability to make decisions, control behaviour, have morals

**puberty** the beginning of adolescence, when the body begins to change from childhood towards adult shape

**REM sleep** rapid eye movement sleep, a deep stage of sleep where most dreams happen. Thought to be important for health and growth. You will normally have four stages of REM each night, though you may not remember the dreams

**schizophrenia** a mental illness involving strong confusion between what is real and what is not

**serotonin** a neurotransmitter responsible for the feeling of content, peaceful happiness; also affects sleep, pain and appetite

**spatial skill** ability to manipulate shapes in your head, to visualize what something will look like the other way round, and to judge distances and angles

**synapse** connection between dendrite of one neuron and axon of another. Actually a tiny gap, rather than a point of touching. Messages cross the synapses and pass to other neurons

**testosterone** a sex hormone found mostly in males, responsible for male body features and some behaviour

**tryptophan** a chemical found in certain foods (e.g. turkey and hot milk) which can make us sleepy

**ventral striatum** part of the basal ganglia. It has a complex (and not well understood) role in both receiving emotional information and regulating aspects of movement

**white matter** most of the brain consists of white matter, lying below the grey matter of the cortex. White matter mostly consists of the long tail-like axons and glial cells

# Author's Note

I am not a scientist by profession. I am certainly not a neuroscientist, psychologist or evolutionary biologist. So how do I dare write this book, which includes aspects of all those disciplines?

How does anyone dare? No scientist understands the human brain fully, and almost certainly none ever will. That's why it's so fascinating. And I am fascinated. That's partly why I dare. My real interest began many years ago, when I was training to teach people with dyslexia. It's when you look at things that can go wrong in the brain, or brain differences, that it becomes so interesting: it begins to make sense. Like being shown the edges of a jigsaw.

Because I am so intrigued by the brain, I have always read about it avidly. I don't have the skills or background knowledge to be a proper scientist, constructing theories and proving or disproving them by primary research. I can only try to understand what the researchers tell us, and to present it clearly, adding my own observations and ideas, and interpretations that make sense to me. Some scientists may think I've done all right – others may not. That's inevitable and, I believe, would also happen if a real scientist had written this book. Scientists disagree with each other too.

I still read everything I can about the teenage brain and am in contact with the scientists doing the cutting edge research. I'm so grateful to them for fuelling my enthusiasm and pointing me towards new information.

Neuroscientists, psychologists and evolutionary biologists look at the brain from different angles. I find each angle equally intriguing. I am also a mother and used to teach teenagers. I now write for teenagers. I feel I understand them. Remarkably, I even was one once.

I think that's why I dare.

**Nicola Morgan speaks to all sorts of groups about aspects of the adolescent brain. She has addressed young people, parents, teachers, medical professionals, social work departments, librarians, adolescent mental health workers and groups, young mental health patients, youth workers, adoption workers, police and community leaders. Do contact her via her website: www.nicolamorgan.com**

# Useful Websites

- About Teen Depression – www.about-teen-depression.com
- Adolescent Development Resources (many topics) www.mhhe.com/socscience/devel/life/devel-4.htm#teen
- American Academy of Child and Adolescent Psychiatry – www.aacap.org
- The Brain Bank – www.thebrainbank.org.uk
- Cardiff University Teenage Alcohol Project – www.cf.ac.uk/socsi/tap
- ChildLine – www.childline.org.uk (also phone free on 0800 11 11, UK only, 24 hours a day)
- Encyclopedia of Psychology (Adolescent Psychology Resources) – www.psychology.org/links/Environment_Behavior_Relationships/Adolescent
- Frontline (Inside the Teenage Brain) – www.pbs.org/wgbh/pages/frontline/shows/teenbrain
- A Guide to Psychology and Its Practice (Adolescent Violence) – www.guidetopsychology.com/ad_viol.htm
- Mind – www.mind.org.uk
- National Sleep Foundation (in USA) – www.sleepfoundation.org
- The Samaritans – www.samaritans.org.uk
- Teens with Problems – www.teenswithproblems.com

# Select Bibliography & Suggestions for Further Reading

- *The Essential Difference* – Simon Baron-Cohen (male/female brain differences)
- *Mapping the Mind* – Rita Carter (particularly good for understanding how the different areas of the brain may work together)
- *The Man Who Tasted Shapes* – Richard Cytowic (synaesthesia, but containing much information about the brain in general)
- *Brain Story* – Susan Greenfield (general overview of the brain, including fascinating insights from things that can go wrong with the brain)
- *The Private Life of the Brain* – Susan Greenfield (a neuroscientist's insight into what is happening in our brains when we experience things like emotion)
- *The Culture of Adolescent Risk-Taking* – Cynthia Lightfoot
- *The Blank Slate* – Steven Pinker (nature versus nurture debate, not just in relation to male/female brain differences)
- *Why Are They So Weird?* – Barbara Strauch (teenage brain, aimed at adult readers)
- *A Bright Red Scream* – by Marilee Strong (self-harming)
- *The Brain Pack* – Ron Van der Meer and Ad Dudink (excellent package of information about the human brain, aimed at young people)

# Notes

1 Emerson Pugh was the computer expert who worked for IBM for 35 years. IBM's chairman, Thomas Watson, said in 1943: "I think there is a world market for maybe five computers."

2 Led by Giacomo Rizzolatti and colleagues at the University of Parma, Italy. See http://psych.colorado.edu/~kimlab/Rizzolatti.annurev.neuro.2004.pdf. A very useful TED talk by VS Ramachandran is here: http://www.ted.com/talks/vs_ramachandran_the_neurons_that_shaped_civilization.html

3 According to Professor Marian Diamond in her book Enriching Heredity.

4 David Hubel and Torsten Wiesel won a Nobel Prize in 1981 for this discovery.

5 This new information about the development of the adolescent brain comes largely from the work of Dr Jay Giedd, a neuroscientist at the National Institute of Mental Health in the United States. For further information about his research and views, start with his interview on the Frontline website at www.pbs.org/wgbh/pages/frontline/shows/teenbrain/interviews/giedd.html

6 This research was carried out by Dr Deborah Yurgelun-Todd of McLean Hospital, Massachusetts.

7 Various interesting papers here: http://sites.google.com/site/blakemorelab/recent_publications Eg "Development of the social brain in adolescence."

8 See the work by Beatrix Luna, Director of the Laboratory of Neurocognitive Development at the University of Pittsburgh, Pennsylvania.

9 For example, "Functional maturation of excitatory synapses in layer 3 pyramidal neurons during postnatal development of the primate prefrontal cortex" Gonzalez-Burgos G, Kroener S, and others – Cereb Cortex. 2008 Mar; 18(3);626-37. Epub 2007 Jun 24.

10 According to research by Mari S. Golub at the California Primate Research Center, University of California at Davis.

11 According to Richard Cytowic's book The Man Who Tasted Shapes.

12 The main researcher whose material I came across, and who is most often quoted in newspaper and other articles, is Dr Mary A. Carskadon, of Brown University and E. P. Bradley Hospital, Providence, Rhode Island.

13 These tests include many studies by Mary Carskadon and her colleagues.

14 A study at Harvard University showed that deep sleep helps the brain store information absorbed the day before; this was reported in USA Today, 27 November 2000.

15   National Sleep Foundation's 2000 Omnibus Sleep in America Poll (OSAP), conducted during October and November 1999.

16   According to Eve Van Cauter, a sleep researcher at the University of Chicago, and reported in Barbara Strauch's book Why Are They So Weird?, p. 174.

17   This study was conducted by Marcos Frank, a neuroscientist at the University of California, San Francisco, and reported in Neuron, April 2001, and widely elsewhere.

18   This study was conducted by Mary Carskadon and her fellow researchers.

19   Time for Bed: Parent-Set Bedtimes Associated with Improved Sleep and Daytime Functioning in Adolescents - Michelle A. Short and others: http://www.ncbi.nlm.nih.gov/pmc/articles/PMC3098947/ AND Sleep in Adolescents: The Perfect Storm by Mary A. Carskadon: PhDhttp://www.ohsu.edu/xd/health/services/doernbecher/research-education/education/residency/upload/Sleep-in-Adolsescents-2011-Carskadon-PED-CLIN-NA.pdf

20   The results of this study were reported in US Today, 27 November 2000 (see also note 10).

21   For example, "Later school start times and Zzzs to A's" – reported by Emily Sohn in the Los Angeles Times, Aug 23, 2010 http://articles.latimes.com/2010/aug/23/health/la-he-school-time-20100823

22   For example, "Earlier Development of the Accumbens Relative to Orbitofrontal Cortex Might Underlie Risk-Taking Behavior in Adolescents" Galvan A. et al Journal of Neuroscience 26. 6885-6892 (2006) http://www.jneurosci.org/content/26/25/6885.full.pdf

23   For example, "Adolescent Development and Juvenile Justice" by Laurence Steinberg Annu. Rev. Clin. Psychol. 2009. 5:47–73 and research by Abigail Baird referred to here: http://www.newscientist.com/article/dn6738

24   "Presence of peers heightens teens' sensitivity to rewards of a risk." ScienceDaily. Temple University (2011, January 28). http://www.sciencedaily.com/releases/2011/01/110128113428.htm

25   According to research by Scott Swartzwelder of Duke University.

26   Scott Swartzwelder, "Differential sensitivity of NMDA receptor-mediated synaptic potentials to ethanol in immature vs. mature hippocampus", Alcoholism: Clinical and Experimental Research, Vol. 19, 1995.

27   Sandra A. Brown, Susan F. Tapert, Eric Granholm and Dean C. Delis, "Neurocognitive functioning of adolescents: effects of protracted alcohol use", Alcoholism: Clinical and Experimental Reaseach, Vol. 24, 2000.

28   Hibell, B et al, 2007 European School Survey Project on Alcohol and Other

Drugs (ESPAD), CAN, Sweden 2009.

29  The research students were Jennifer Connellan and Anna Batki – the face
    was Jennifer's!

30  This research was carried out by Dr Jay Giedd at the National Institute of
    Mental Health.

31  This theory was suggested by anthropologist Barry Bogin of the University
    of Michigan-Dearborn, and described in the New Scientist, 6 March 1993.

32  This research was carried out by Professor Michelle Ehrlich and Dr Ellen
    Unterwald at Thomas Jefferson University, Philadelphia.

33  Charles A. Nelson, "Neural plasticity and human development: the role of
    early experience in sculpting memory systems", Developmental Science,
    3:2, 2000.

34  M. C. Diamond, D. Krech and M. R. Rosenzweig, "The effects of an enriched
    environment on the histology of the rat cerebral cortex", Journal of
    Comparative Neurology, 123, 1964.

Because many pieces of research have become so widely quoted in
newspapers, the Internet, books and all written material, it is sometimes
difficult or impossible to find the primary source. Sometimes, with the
best intention, I have not always succeeded. Some research results have
simply become general knowledge and I have never intentionally ignored
anyone's work.

# Index

*Page numbers in **bold** refer to the glossary*